Writing the Land: Northeast

Published by Human Error Publishing
Paul Richmond
www.humanerrorpublishing.com
paul@humanerrorpublishing.com

ISBN: 978-1-948521-79-6

Front & Back Covers:
Apis by Martin Bridge and design by Martin Bridge
https://www.thebridgebrothers.com
Interior book design: Lis McLoughlin

Writing the Land: Northeast

Edited by Lis McLoughlin, PhD
with a foreword by Tom Butler

Published by
Human Error Publishing
Wendell, MA

Foreword

Let's be honest: Writing the land is impossible. The land writes itself, sings the song of itself in languages older than words, in creak and croak and thunderclap, in wail of loonsong, murmur of leaf rustle, insect hum, wolf howl. The languages of people, various and rich but so new in the pageant of life, are wholly inadequate to capture the land's music.

But . . . attempting to write the land is noble. And delightful. Perhaps even essential. To add our compositions, imperfect and incomplete as they may be, to the land's great symphony, joining our human song to the chorus of voices helps us make sense of our place and purpose in the diversity of life.

Our moment in time, with its entwined crisis of climate chaos and ecological unraveling offers up a continuous mix of horrors, current and anticipated, to contemplate. The land, however, despite its sufferings, offers daily an antidote to despair. What better way to avoid forethought of grief than to greet one's wild cousins, hemlock and moose, and acknowledge the wind, moon, and sun? To be cheered by flower, waved at by leaf, sung to by warbler—these daily blessings ground us.

In a spirit of reciprocity, many of us work to safeguard the ground that grounds us. This work, in our culture, has come to be known as "conservation," a term encompassing a wide array of actions with legal and ethical foundations, and which can permanently protect specific places. The parks and wilderness areas we treasure, the undammed rivers, the natural habitats supporting wildlife, the scenic vistas of unmarred country . . . where such beauty and wildness remain it is generally not because the forces of development haven't yet arrived but because people who loved the land used their own wild and precious lives resisting those forces. And were successful.

In America's fractious body politic, the land trust movement is remarkably nonpolitical, bipartisan, even hopeful. It's a vanishingly rare area of civic life that attracts people from across the political spectrum, whose interests range from conserving local farms and timberlands to setting aside great swaths of the planet from human domination and letting nature *rewild*—that is to say, *heal*, places degraded by human exploitation. The commonality within this broad movement is devotion to the land.

If expanding the number of people who feel this devotion and express it through conservation efforts is crucial to a beautiful future for humanity and all our relations on Earth (and I do believe it is), how might that come to pass? How will we win hearts and minds to the righteous cause of wildness? Surely the land's intrinsic beauty and wild life—and human interpreters of these attributes—will play central roles in rewilding ourselves, a fundamental task if we are to regain responsible citizenship in the biotic community.

In this urgent work of interpretation, celebration, and reconnection we have much to learn from land lovers of various kinds—amateur naturalists, formally trained ecologists, community elders, organic farmers, low-impact loggers, wilderness champions. And *poets*.

Yes, poets, the concise storytellers, armed with visions. The voices of courage that sometimes, when the stars and words align, perform the shaman's task, guiding us to look beyond surfaces and tap our individual sense of wonder. Thanks always to these guides who see our fellow members in the land community and recognize them as family. Who in the favor of their poetry remind us that Earth returns our love.

———Tom Butler, Senior Fellow, Northeast Wilderness Trust
Summer 2021, foothills of Vermont's Green Mountains

Introduction

Into My Own
by Robert Frost

One of my wishes is that those dark trees,
So old and firm they scarcely show the breeze
Were not, as 'twere, the merest mask of gloom,
But stretched away unto the edge of doom.
I should not be withheld but that some day
Into their vastness I should steal away,
Fearless of ever finding open land,
Or highway where the slow wheel pours the sand.
I do not see why I should e'er turn back,
Or those should not set forth upon my track
To overtake me, who should miss me here
And long to know if still I held them dear.
They would not find me changed from him they knew—
Only more sure of all I thought was true.

Before Writing the Land, there was Thinking the Land. Enjoyable, but not quite efficacious. In my off-grid cottage in a mature hemlock forest in Northfield, Massachusetts for years I contemplated the land. And as I walked those acres with Robert Frost, feeling his cadences in my hiking feet, I knew that words and land wrote each other. And it occurred to me, that in this way land contributes to its own protection; that land speaks, and that Nature poets are trained to hear those voices.

So what does it matter, this conversation, asked the activist in me? In a time when land needs all the help it can get just to survive, how can poets help the land that we love protect itself? The answer is through land trusts. Land Trusts are the protectors of land with boots, GPS, a force of volunteers and even—if needed—lawyers, land trusts defend land against the highway, the strip mall, industrial agriculture that depletes, and the thoughtless clearcut. And simultaneously open land to plants, creatures, and often, poets.

Through this partnership, Thinking the Land became Writing the Land, which in this pilot year was comprised of 11 land trusts and 36 separate lands, and has since evolved to include over 100 poets with almost 50 land trusts and other partners for next year. I am so grateful to these poets, and our collaborators for hearing the voices that surround us, and for their faith in the project to spread the word to others. Writing the Land participants are honored to be doing essential work for our lands. By pairing poets with protected lands, we offer ourselves as a conduit for the land to speak, to sing, to cry out, to comfort.

Just as each poem is an individual's interpretation of the voices they hear, each land trust's chapter reflects their unique approach to the work of land protection. Together they tell a story about a different journey than the one our mainstream culture is on—a journey to explore, preserve, and nurture the dream of a vastness into which we can lose—and find—ourselves.

—*6/16/21*
L. McLoughlin
Hemlock House
Northfield, MA

NB. "Into My Own" by Robert Frost is now in the public domain. It was originally published in *A Boy's Will* (Henry Holt, 1915)

TABLE OF CONTENTS

NORTHEAST

WILDERNESS
TRUST

NORTHEAST WILDERNESS TRUST

New England & New York

At Northeast Wilderness Trust, we do conservation differently. We are the only regional land trust that can promise every acre we protect today will be an old-growth forest of tomorrow.

In the Northeastern United States, places where nature can evolve and thrive without human interference are rare. But together, we can change this. On lands protected by the Wilderness Trust, plants and animals, fungi and insects, water and soil are all free to be exactly as they are. Wild nature belongs in this corner of the world and it offers benefits to people unmatched by human-dominated lands.

-Eagle Mountain Wilderness Preserve-Sylvia Karman
-Alder Stream Wilderness Preserve-David Crews
-Muddy Pond Wilderness Preserve-Kathy Kremins
-Binney Hill Wilderness Preserve-Rachelle Parker

Peregrine Falcon at Eagle Mountain by Brendan Wiltse

Eagle Mountain Wilderness Preserve

Eagle Mountain Wilderness is in the northern foothills of the Adirondacks, a geologically young mountain range at five to ten million years old. The preserve is part of the ancestral land of the Kanien'kehá:ka—or the Mohawk nation. I hiked into Eagle Mountain Wilderness for the first time in October 2020 along the remnants of an old logging road reminding me of the history of the land and our relationship with it. Eagle Mountain Wilderness has much to offer about that relationship and how we can restore it. Since then I have had the good fortune to return to the preserve. The following poems represent my attempt to reflect on what wilderness can share when I pay attention.   -Sylvia Karman, 6/23/21

Hiking Eagle Mountain Wilderness
by Sylvia Karman

> *Imagine walking through a richly inhabited world*
> *of Birch people, Bear people, Rock people...*
> *-Robin Wall Kimmerer,* Braiding Sweetgrass

By what name do the trees know us?
They speak in balsam scents, their breezy brogues swish & creak,
birch & maple crowns cast sunlight coins that wink

my name along the logging road long surrendered
to pioneers whose seeds tag my sleeves & the wolfish drape
of my shepherd mix's tail—they mark us chance in motion

& settle on a giant's fist of till near a pond where the shepherd spies a
                                                              beaver
          Tsianì:to   le castor   der Biber   Castor canadensis
whose gaze returns our marvel before he turns to ripples, water covers
                                             him sleek in sleek reflecting

the mountain—her south facing ice-plucked cliffs shelter raptor
nations—she extends her wild
lap to the winged & mineraled, the rooted & roaming, to any called to
wonder & become
possibility.

The following two poems are written in a Japanese poetry form known as tanka *which typically consists of 31 syllables: the first and third lines have five syllables each, and the other lines each have seven syllables.-SK*

Northern Flicker (Yellow Shafted) Meets Cooper's Hawks
by Sylvia Karman

Gold feathers, coal tips
fanned at birch roots, offering.
Hawk shadows cross paths.
A breeze lifts the retrices
of those in flight, in service.

One Myotis Lucifugus
by Sylvia Karman

Lone mouse-eared brown bat
skirrs dusk, feeding on echoes.
Absence chases her.
Beneath her mammalian wings
trail cauldrons of white-nosed ghosts.

Alder Stream by Shelby Perry

Alder Stream Wilderness Preserve

Alder Stream in Atkinson, ME—what is also ancestral land of Penobscot Abenaki peoples—contains extensive groves of wild reproducing chestnut trees. This poem includes italicized lines from Lauret Savoy and Masanobu Fukuoka, and is part of a longer sequence for Northeast Wilderness Trust. This poem was also published in Wild Northeast.   *-David Crews, 12/20*

Alder Stream
by David Crews

The colors are turning

here, in the most heavily logged state of the nation's
history

stretches of I-95 go without trees

I look at the road atlas and see highways that network
northward snakelike boughs and branches

paper birch, gray birch, black birch

In the distance big mountains loom where the AT nears
the end of its two-thousand mile pilgrimage

here, in the Maine woods—Abenaki ancestral lands

American beech, balsam fir, white cedar

How and why do we know what we know?

Some say this land contains the largest grove of wild
reproducing chestnuts

sits at the farthest northern reaches of chestnut habitat

here, at the ecotone

how light can I make myself?

Stepping through leaves spiked burrs rest just underfoot—
some dried and brown, some open, some still green

encasing delicate seed

these trees are smaller and more sick than I imagined

Blight of the American chestnut in the last hundred years
includes the loss of more than three billion trees

infected by a pathogen that colonizes a wound in the
bark

red oak, white pine, tamarack

The grove of chestnut sits atop a slight ridge just over
the Piscataquis river

contraptions of netting here and there to catch falling
debris—part of a study

how this land too some think proves the farthest reaches
of the blight

Penobscot river, Piscataquis river, Alder stream

alder of the genus *Alnus*—flowering plant, of the birch

from Old English *alor*, proto-Germanic root *aliso*, and
el- for red, brown

speckled alder, red maple, striped maple

Some researchers claim the only way to restore chestnut
populations—genetically engineered species

A single step away from the source can only lead astray

Up close and without vista the woods look imperfect

broken branches, fallen and rotting trees, half-open burrs,
and fresh scat pressed and smeared on a rock

how I am drawn to fields of seeding milkweed

their pods opening to soft, silky, starlike filaments—
the coma lifting into wind

O teach me to love the mutilated world

Scientists say it is not uncommon in evolutionary history
for a species to give another species a gene

when a genetically engineered father tree is planted near
a wild mother, half the chestnut yield will carry

a blight tolerant trait

at what point will the wild chestnut be gone?

quaking aspen, American elm, black ash

So it is told that a squirrel once could travel Georgia
to Maine on only the branches of chestnut trees

Castanea dentata—American chestnut

My steps bushwhacking here are delicate for these
chestnut trees are not big

leaves now quite familiar: elongated, serrated, still
very green

I see them everywhere scattered about the dense forest

illumined in pockets of sunlight

what if I did not know to maneuver the burrs?

What living creatures does each step press into
the earth?

How obvious this love for birds someone once said
—they need no trails

to be feather-light and adrift to thermals

I could love the mutilated world

The chestnut contains over 30,000 genes of DNA—
researchers want to give it one

peacekeeping enzyme that protects the tree from a
harmful acid

I look on Alder stream and its beaver dams and wonder

which trees are mountain alder, which are speckled

these woods speak a language of water and light

and I yearn to translate what's lost

where to praise means to save, and to preserve keeps
trees from dying

still, I know so little of life's reckonings

The memory of what we found shapes me still

black spruce, eastern hemlock, American chestnut

Water lily and bee at Muddy Pond by Natalia Boltukhova

Garter snake at Muddy Pond by Natalia Boltukhova

Muddy Pond Wilderness Preserve

Pine Barrens Plainsong
by Kathy Kremins

Will they know us, Muddy Pond?
Will the sky see our dance?
Pale reddish pine needles
nestle in late winter hardness
like land I walked as a child
in Jersey Pine Barrens fragrance.

Will I know you, Muddy Pond?
Will the wind taste the same?
Stretched across stolen land
ancestor voices vibrate, Lenape south
Wampanoag north, across land
burdened with history, gather, honor

sacred space swirls with a breathing
across miles, boundary-less, gentian reaches
pulls me to pitch pine and oak
coastal plain pond, reclaim the sweetness.
Will you know me, Muddy Pond?
Will the earth hear this hymn?

Night Pools
by Kathy Kremins

Why am I always so excited with anticipation of that first time:
first look, lingering, and the first touch,
drawing nearer to the moisture and
the sound of my own breath?

Seeing and listening with attention has taken me lifetimes, too long.
But you lead me through the woods deliberately,
quietly guiding me deeper into the dark,
closer to the peepers and tree frogs,
vernal pool after vernal pool.

Why do I seem to be stuck or lost, hesitating before entering the woods?
No light, no compass, no desire: a pattern of repetitive gestures,
a dullness of intuition, a blundering and
fumbling of a creative ache...

I hear you exhale and whisper what might be my name as you reach into
                                                        the net.
The spotted salamander struggles, but only momentarily and settles
with a firm grip onto your thumb. I open my hands to you and
a shiver ripples through me. I want that first moment
over and over again, knowing what I know now,
how to touch more lightly, slowly, sighing
at your mysterious, magnificent form,
holding you, tenderly,
gently, in awe.

Hum a Home
Kathy Kremins

Much is made of late winter
light how the angle
of March sun darkens the sky
into azure blue
so diving into the pine
forest splashes solitude
reflected off Muddy Pond.
On next visit, Spring
will perform Her symphony
opening sonata accompanied
by toads, frogs, insects
salamanders in vernal
pools, then andante
gentle emergence
wildflowers, painted turtles.

But for today, long shadows
of winter are my companions.
The sound of my boots
on fallen needles, pine cones, rocks
mud, oak leaves under stubborn snow.
The pond glimmer stops me
frozen with stillness, then
the beating of my heart
rhythm of my breath.
When you hear the quiet
don't fill it with words
or noise. Let the geese call
and the wind answer.
Gather the notes inside where
silent nature hums a home.

Moose pair at Binney Hill by Daryl Burtnett

Binney Hill Wilderness Preserve

There Were No Yellow Triangles, Just Da Moss
by Rachelle Parker

Could a been moose dung
A spring, waitin' to be drunk
Maple leaves gorged on early snow
Ferns sproutin' from underneath a big ole rock
Spores on a birch what look like Chesapeake oysters
Starlings makin' due with this new nest, home
New bugs thirstin' for your hide, too
Echoes of momma callin' out
Black spruce
Silver trout
Cool air
Deep breathes
Scabbed fingers, from the cutter, picking…
Blueberries

On The North Side of the Juniper
by Rachelle Parker

Look for the half frozen pond.
Mosses will be lush and pea green.

Birds and otters and snakes, sing your arrival,
chirping and splashing and slithering.

Stems and twigs in their mouths
follow the beaver until he disappears

behind a waterfall. It will be dry there.
The darkness of a cave will cradle you,

move you to tears and sleep. A peek of
morning lights your way through dewed grasses

to the blueberries. Fill your kerchief with wildness.
Munch these new fruits, let their juices

run through your raisin'd skin until plump.
You bursting at the seams and left bare.

Go when the silver fins beckon you.
They know how deep down the earth is.
They have laid eggs there.

Slowly enter the pond. Slowly dip your head
under. Slowly release the dust from bitter
wounds, from thick keloids at the wrists
and ankles, from the mark under your eye
left by a fetterbush.

Cleansed, sit on the bank, look at your reflection
See the return of the gazelle.

Do Not Look The Journey in the Eye: A Haibun
by Rachelle Parker

When you arrive, you know that faith is baby steps. It is running
with dogs at your heels and jumping into a pond without knowing
how to swim. Strokes come from instinct. Taking in air when you can
until you are back, safely, on the land. Your flax dress clinging to skin
weary of a season change. Feet will know the ground is cooler. Lungs
will know the air is cooler. Blood will run cooler. Your grandmothers'
grandmothers have whispered. A black spruce will offer its trunk
and branch for rest and shade and a collection of seeds. Blueberries
will be easy pickings for fingers scarred by a cutter. Loopers will
die off without the overseer of tobacco.

> Run to cooler land
> Loopers no longer hold you back
> Grandmothers know what's ahead

New Hampshire Audubon

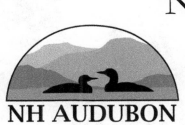

NH AUDUBON

Concord, NH

Protecting New Hampshire's natural environment for wildlife and for people

Founded in 1914 with an original focus on protecting and restoring migratory bird populations decimated by hunting and collection in the late nineteenth and early twentieth centuries, today's NH Audubon provides:

- Environmental education programs throughout the state
- Statewide conservation research and wildlife monitoring
- Protection of nearly 10,000 acres of wildlife habitat in 39 sanctuaries
- Environmental public policy and science-based advocacy

A nonprofit, statewide membership organization independent of the National Audubon Society, NH Audubon operates three centers (in Auburn, Concord, and Hebron). *www.nhaudubon.org*

-Dahl Wildlife Sanctuary
-Cheryl Savageau
-Dan Close
-Katheryn Hagopian Berry

Dahl Wildlife Sanctuary Trail Map

SANCTUARY & TRAIL INFORMATION

Please enjoy yourself, stay on the trial, do not pick flowers or plants, and be careful of poison ivy.

1) Pine Trail: From the trailhead kiosk, the Pine Trail parallels Rt. 16 to a turnaround. The trail wanders uphill along the ridge of the esker and through a second-growth upland pine forest. Round trip ½ mile.

2) Silver Maple Loop Trail: From the trailhead kiosk take the road down the hill to the trail junction where there is an interpretive sign. From this junction, take a left onto the Silver Maple Trail. The field on your right was once farmed but now is being managed as a habitat for upland and nesting birds and a variety of wildlife. Stay on the trail as there are still remnants of barbed wire along the trail edge. The canopy here is dominated by silver maple, with other species such as sugar maple, white ash and American Elm.

As you reach the interpretative sign, the low wetland in front of you is called a meander scar, where the Saco River once flowed. The interpretive sign explains the diversity of the floodplain and how it supports false nettle, sensitive fern and other herbaceous plants, as well as habitat for denning mammals and nesting birds, and provides vernal pools for amphibians.

Continuing on this trail will bring you to the trail junction where you can bear left on the Beach Trail or turn right back to the trailhead. The Silver Maple loop is ½ mile.

3) For the **Beach Trail** go straight ahead at the trail junction near the interpretive sign onto the Field Trail. The trail passes an oxbow to your right where mallards and mergansers may be seen, but be quiet as they are sensitive to intruders. You will pass over a gravel stone bridge. To your left, a wetland overflow has been created and when dry, paw prints of deer, moose, bear, and fox may be seen.

The field to the left contains a bat box and kestrel box, as well as 13 bird boxes where blackcapped chickadees, house wrens, and tree swallows nest. The grasses in the field provide cover and habitat for wildlife such as mice and voles. Looking across the water, a large colony of Eastern painted turtles makes their home. The trail comes to a junction at the tree line.

The Silver Maple Trail makes a loop around the field to the left. For the Beach Trail, go across the brook bed and into the woods and bear left.

The Beach Trail runs parallel to the Saco River and ends at the cobble barren (beach). Looking across at the river bank, you may see holes where bank swallows make their home. At the cobble barren you may see belted kingfisher and common mergansers with ducklings. Along the forest edge of the beach is a globally rare community of hudsonia – silverling, which is currently known only on channel barrens along the Saco River in NH and Maine.

The Audubon property ends at the large DAHL sign near the edge of the woods. The rest of the beach is owned by the town of North Conway.

Retracing the trail you may notice the young trees with angular cuts close to the ground. This is the work of beavers that cut the trees and drag them into the river and to their lodges. As you follow the trail notice the debris above your head. It was deposited there in the flood of 2011 when there was over 7 feet of water throughout the sanctuary. A number of silver maple trees were uprooted and the bird boxes were filled with mud. But it is a floodplain forest and that is expected. The Beach Trail round trip to the cobble barren is 1 mile.

River Barren View by Phil Brown

Dahl Wildlife Sanctuary

Thirteen Moons on the Saco
by Cheryl Savageau

i
it's snowing big flakes
birds fly over the flood plain
summer on their wings

ii
three pairs of mallards
the green and blue of the males
iridescent

iii
brown spots on white breast
sandpiper walks the wet beach
among red maple seedlings

iv
five soft thin needles
green on the branches
copper on the floor

v
in the cobble barren
green lobes of lichens on rocks
furry beach heather flowers yellow

vi
kayaks on river
teenagers swimming off rocks
green dragonfly

vii
loons float down the slow river
in the banks, swallows nesting

viii
in the tall grass
butterflies hover over milkweed
bear cub tumbles into blueberries

ix
eagle black against the sky
the calls of bluejays and crows
white birch yellow leaves

x
dusk
red leaves falling
moose wades in

xi
geese calling
from their arrow in the sky
chill wind

xii
in a forest of grey branches
the only color
is the red of the cardinal

xiii
morning, open ice
opal-faced otter
gobbles fish
then dives

Dahl Ephemerals by Phil Brown

The Saco at Dahl Sanctuary, North Conway, New Hampshire
by Dan Close

In the spring the Saco roars and tears its way along its ancient bed.
Fed by the fires of the sun, these crystals of the final snows
            cascade down from presidential heights where nothing grows
            but rock and ice and winter.
Its waters carry diamonds in its ripples
            that shimmer in the springtime sun,
            and also boulders, tree trunks ripped
            from savaged banks upstream,
And it can carry danger.

But on a placid summer day like this
With fairish breezes blowing all around
It rests, and nodding to the trees
That make their stand upon its sandy banks
It slows, and visits with the forest.

Two kinds of beings, each
With its own sense of time, they greet each other.
Long have these two forces of the earth been neighbors –
The river never knowing time except as headlong rush;
The forest knowing every single year
            inscribed in its concentric circles...
And yet they take one of our aeons
To meet together, before each of them is gone –

The river, turbulently philosophizing where it is,
And where it is going, and whence it came to be,
Until it tumbles to the vastness of the sea;

The forest, glowing silent in its green,
Crumbling placidly into the mists of time
But leaving something of itself behind.

And yet, they speak, or meet at least.
On this fine day enjoying, the two of them together,
Everything about the earth
Under the sun of summertime.

The Red-Shouldered Hawk at the Dahl Sanctuary
by Dan Close

The red-shouldered hawk flies high above   (Kee-rak!)
By dawn, by midday light, by dusky twilight,
Up above all, high in the sky
He flies.
Far up in the sky
His keen eye on his flocks below,
In case any creature needs help, you know.

Chipmunks and froggies and small snakes – Beware!
Better look up and get out of there...
Into the woods, into the goo,   (*Kee-rah!*)
Stay out of reach whatever you do!
A willowing of wingtips, a flick of the tail,
A quick hawkeye flutter, and down he sails –
Sudden, he drops on his prey below
A puff of dust, and the chipmunk goes
Flying off to Red Hawk's aerie,
High in the branches of the highest ash tree.

Safe to come out now, for a bit,
The warbler, the bobolink, bunting and tit
Breathe a sigh of relief, then gather their songs,
And join their fellows in sing-alongs
While holding, however, their collective breath
For the sight of the shadow that will bring them rest.

Riding the thermal high up in the sky –
A soft-pillowed perch ever so high.   (Kee-RAK!)
The cry goes into ten thousand ears
As it has for a million years.
The Red Hawk is up once again in the sky
Along with his mate, this time – (Kee-rak-kee Kee-rai!)

The Searchers at the Dahl Sanctuary
by Dan Close

Giant old sugar maple, silver maple, white ash
floodplain forest
cobble beach down by the Saco river
a world apart
five trails to choose from
misty morning
birds, butterflies, toads,
mosquitoes for swatting and deet
which trail shall we take
all of them before this day is through
warbler, bunting, sandpiper by the shore,
merganser on the river
bluebird, tree swallow, blue-gray gnatcatcher
house wren, chickadee
barred owl
twenty-six species we got today, kids
not to mention that old red-shouldered hawk
flying high in the sky, watching us
like we were hairless bears searching for berries.

Untitled by Phil Brown

Landtrust
by Katherine Hagopian Berry

This is the magic
you walk the land
take nothing, not even your eyes
you must close them
until there is no looking
only darkness like an open hand.

This is the magic
you place one foot in front of another
trails blazed on your bones
or even wandering
some iron in the blood
leads you safehome.

This is the magic
the treasured stick.
the mica stone,
above you sky unrolls
a maryshawl of blue,
to hold them.

This is the magic
every lightray, pressed
to your heart like a lover,
every newbud leaf,
like you, it will fall
like you, it will come back changed.

Before we reach the Skelton Dam
by Katherine Hagopian Berry

Above the curse line, in New Hampshire
the Saco is a different river, so mild
kayakers drift, their music, paddles
like white flags across bent knees.

On the margin of the cobble barren
I can imagine a different beginning
bark, brigantine, ketch, sloop, seeking
dawnshore, palms over open hearts.

Below my feet the stones
in the shallows are all the colors
of human hands, water brushes
them one along the other, ever gentling.

I wade in. Imagine curses
lifting, knives, falls, broken
bodies sated, blood enough
for blood, even my blond son.

Walking back the trail, caterpillars
are melting from every hemlock, pinetree,
seeking redemption, I imagine some bright genus
reconciliation unfolding like wings.

At the LLBean I ask them
browntail moth, they say, invasive
a menace, flamerash, poison, no mercy,
they destroy everything they touch.

Day before her birthday; Dahl Wildlife Sanctuary
by Katherine Hagopian Berry

On the silver maple trail, *we*
wonder have we seen it all, *realize*
we have forgotten the rare cobble barren, *that*
longed for habitat, hairy hudsonia, silverling, *vegetation*
dragonnamed, but the sky isn't *clearing*
stray raindrops, open shoes, all untied, it *is*
easier to circle, *a*
fragile spider, half orbiting *messy*
nest box poles, barbed wire, *transition*
meadow, the falsenettle, mayflower, bellwort *and*
you are almost twelve, taking selfies, *visually*
flinching, worry contorting your eyes, are they *unattractive*
your legs like a fiddlehead poised to unfurl? So *we*
learn to notice the gold in our hair, cease to *apologize for*
nearsight, the way it forces attention, *the*
truth is our whole *short-term*
preoccupation with *appearance*
is nonsense anyway, I tell you, *we*
are alone in the field, there *are*
creatures in stickdens huddling close, *glad*
of their dark bodies. I have saved only one picture, *you*
like a raptor, listening for water, have *chosen*
profile, birchbark, floodplain, thicket *to*
remember our *visit*
capture the cloudsky, the swale, the meander scar, *us.*

Untitled by Phil Brown

We envision a world where people lead happier and healthier lives by connecting with nature and finding inspiration to conserve and enjoy the environment they love.

Through our lands and programs, NH Audubon's members, staff, and volunteers promote a deeper understanding of the natural world, and provide enduring opportunities to experience wildlife and their habitats.

UPPER VALLEY

LAND TRUST

Upper Valley
Land Trust

Hanover, NH

Working in 45 New Hampshire and Vermont towns that make up the Upper Valley, UVLT conserves, protects and stewards our region's lands for the health and resilience of nature and people.

From its founding in 1987, UVLT has brought together the diverse skills and perspectives of Upper Valley people to create effective conservation solutions while simultaneously strengthening the fabric of human community. This neighborly way of working, where all people are welcomed to shape priorities and participate in the stewardship of conserved places, remains our core identity today.

Over the past three decades, we've conserved more than 540 parcels encompassing 55,000 acres -- working farms, forested ridges, wildlife habitat, water resources, trails and scenic landscapes. UVLT owns Conservation Areas and Nature Preserves, manages hundreds of miles of trails, and hosts school programs and academic research on conserved lands.

UVLT is creating a future where people feel a personal connection to land and share a sense of stewardship for nature as an essential aspect of community life; of local food, clean water and resilient forests; where wild nature will thrive and residents will hike and paddle, birdwatch, wander, and teach their children about nature.

-True's Ledges-Christopher Locke
-The Dismal-Jessica Purdy
-Up on the Hill-Hope Jordan

True's Ledges by Megan Chapman

True's Ledges

True's Ledges
Lebanon, NH
by Christopher Locke

Its name incites hope, a chance
to lift this year's shadow, but your
dress shoes nearly falter, the trail
shattered in oak leaves, November
air so raw even the saplings bow
inconsolable. We stand at the rim,
a gorge perfect for young love to fling
itself over after nobody understands,
and I smile at the pageantry, thankful
I've forgotten such claims. I manage
my way down, careful in my footing
as I shake rainwater from young pine,
prickling my neck and my hair. I
discover a white sluice of roaring
channeled between rocks, unending,
mist rising like prayer until I spy you
above, looking down over what is left,
both truth and memory between us
and every landscape we've left behind.

A Return
by Christopher Locke

Wind falters against a boulder,

pushes around the immovable

and me as I busy the shoreline

with quick steps, pebbles

spitting underfoot. I avoid

puddles and leap the scribbled

runoff. A cardinal speaks

up, his deep slur a confession

of nothing until his mate calls

back, ruffles a bough in her

everyday brown. They criss

cross ahead of me, darting

between sunlight punching holes

through the mist, the male's red

coat so electric you'd believe

his song was written in blood.

True's Ledges by Doug Brown

In 1960, the swimming hole at True's Ledges was described by the Saturday Evening Post: "True's Brook, a short-lived but energetic mountain stream which surrenders after several miles to the southward-coursing Connecticut River has kindly scooped out this natural basin." The subject of a local fundraising campaign, this two-acre area was conserved and is now owned by the City of Lebanon.

The Dismal

Trail Map Study
by Jessica Purdy

You don't have to know what the moss is named
or know how many boards it took to make the bridge.
You don't have to know which book to open
or where to find the light of your curiosity.
If only there were a way to portal yourself
to the woods when you need them. Leave
behind those who would try to stop your finding out,
try to discourage your study of leaves: what shade
of green; pattern of veins; what pink flower buds?
That you might want to make someone feel better
by finding medicinal properties in the wildflowers.
That the home you have found here in New Hampshire
is the first place you are learning to breathe.
You don't need a manual for this kind of living.

The Dismal at Pressey Brook, in Hanover, is 240 acres of wetlands and forest donated to UVLT in 2018. Harte and Ann Crow and their sons loved the streams, woods and wild places bestowing the "Dismal" name in honor of the more famous swamp.

Dismal Bridge by Doug Brown

At the Dismal at Pressey Brook Conservation Land
by Jessica Purdy

Annoyance in spring, gnats in my eyes. Forgetting
bug spray and sunglasses.

Loud cars. Packs of motorcycles
needing attention. Popping their exhaust.

Exhaustion. Not getting in position
to film the eagle before it flies away.

People who leave the toilet seat up.
Being awakened by noise. Ticks.

Anything sticky on the floor.
Ants on the floor. Hot flashes.

All this could be solved with a waterfall
in the Dismal at Pressey Brook. Arriving

at the trail, our long-awaited destination,
it starts downpouring.

The slow sizzle like hamburger in a hot pan.
The crunch of old twigs underfoot.

A fallen tree dips its fingers in, combs the running water.
A sieve. A spider web between branches.

I consider how the dead tree's intrusion
ruins the waterfall's perfection. But then see

how its branches are like this woman's body, eager
to rest, trailing her fingers, letting the water's silk

run, asking so little from her world?
I cannot make the waterfall run, but I can dip my fingers in.

Mossy stones, emerald green pillows soft
against the cheek of silk brown water.

What if the tree grasped the boulder in its hand
and held it in its palm; grew together as the land shifted?

How much bloodroot can blossom in two weeks?
The dye can color our clothes, our blankets.

What if we didn't have to worry; that the water would never stop
running, falling; that the sound would never end, leave us bereft?

Even the ticks, those hangers-on, can be seen, picked off.
Layers of clothing can be put on in chill, shed in heat.

The air's changing temperature rapid as mountain storms.
We can be stopped by the ticking of rain falling in vernal pools.

A big black dog crashing out from the underbrush looks us in the eye,
stops moving, then charges

back down the trail, its red collar flashing brightly like a beacon home.

☼

Swamp Milkweed by Jason Berard

Having Visited
by Jessica Purdy

I want to go back to the Dismal to see
what has happened since I left it last.

Did they take away the tree that fell across
the waterfall like a woman fainting

in a silent film? The back of her
hand across her forehead, her fingers

trailing in the spill. Water striders
walking on the surface like miracles. The logger

who came to take her away, did he have
wide hands, thick fingers? Did the dog

who emerged from the brush find its owner?
Did the car with the windows down get

soaked with rain? What flowers bloom
there now? Daisies? Queen Anne's Lace?

What vines have crept up the trunks
of trees to choke them; is it called bittersweet?

They reach for the sun with the tips
of their leaves. I want to smell the air

there after it rains, to have heard thunder
and run to the edge of the water on a

cushion of needles. I want to see the boulder
held in the palm of the tree's roots, hear

the brief calls of birds I can't name, hear
the water as it glides over the rocks slippery

with moss, green as good health and soft
as a kiss. I want to go again with my husband

and we'll strip off our clothes, shake
the ticks off, share some water and

leave our review of the destination
hanging private in the air there. No question

we found our way in and we'll find
our way back out. I want to be grateful

I don't know what it's like to have never
been here, to have loved like that.

Dismal Landscape by Doug Brown

Up on the Hill

Father's Day, 2021
by Hope Jordan

Rows of corn whiffle in the heated breeze

remind me of the muck workers you got to know

summertimes when you ran the register at my uncle's store

on the lake road corner. Those men who spent

the night on our couches and floor. Here the mylar

balloon made its pilgrimage for who knows how

many miles carried by hot air,

collapsed at the base of cornstalks, a bright red

and white Congratulations! Father's Day.

The old wooden gate rots alongside the road.

The new one's shiny metal, and closed.

Up on the Hill Conservation Area in Charlestown was once two farms. The families of Chris and Harvey Hill cared for the land for decades. The couple honored the history of stewardship by donating 1084 acres of fields and woods to UVLT in 2016. Up on the Hill is a working landscape where farming and forestry are ongoing, where UVLT manages a food pantry garden and where exploring for wildflowers and monarch butterflies is welcomed.

Photo: Up on the Hill by Doug Brown (right)

Unoccupied
by Hope Jordan

but signs of habitation – cultivated rows
of corn, just a giant grass, and meadows
upon meadows. My first eastern kingbird
shakes his tyrant head. Tyrant flycatcher.
Fire-engine-tie-father. Here shadows
occupy outbuildings. Here the champion beech
tree contains microclimates. A beechnut
clunks to the ground, green and hard. High
on nitrogen, invasives tendril into the paths.
Beneath the blue and white sky a base
of ferns lifts daisies, purple clover, black-eyed
Susans, all gazing up & into the sun.

Eye Socket Pond, Midsummer

by Hope Jordan

Where milkweed blossoms curl in clusters,

pink confections served on leaves

shaped like platters. First the sound

of a bullfrog, then another, then another, a mid-year

mid-day call and response, here

is where the earth turns, right

here we are suspended between all

that was and all that will be,

here is the father still alive,

still going up the hill to hay

the meadow, to plow the field, to harvest

the forest. Here is an old spiderweb

strung between stalks. Standing timber.

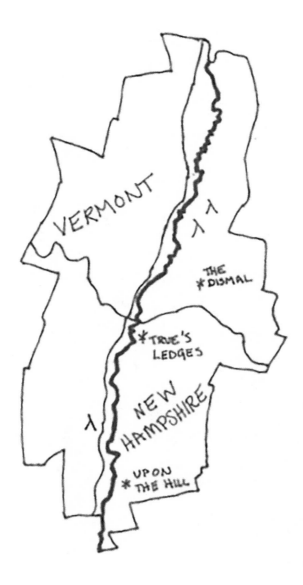

Upper Valley Map by Alison Marchione

Monadnock Conservancy

Keene, NH

The Monadnock region. It's nearly 800 square miles of forests, hills, rivers, lakes, and mountains. Since 1989, the Monadnock Conservancy, together with willing landowners, has permanently conserved 240 properties totaling 21,000 acres in 29 towns throughout southwestern New Hampshire. Our work is rooted in supporting and embracing the connections between the well-being of people and the region's unique rural character.

As an accredited land conservation trust, we accomplish our mission by acquiring land and permanent conservation agreements, by caring for these lands, by creating and maintaining recreational trails, and by building partnerships to prioritize nature, land, and water for the benefit of all—people, plants, and wildlife—now and in the future.

Together, protecting forever the land we love

-John and Rosemarie Calhoun Family Forest-Rodger Martin
-Whittemore Island-Alice B. Fogel
-Cunningham Pond Conservation Area-Ann B. Day
-Chamberlain Conservation Area-Swift Corwin

Come Explore!

The four properties numbered on this map are the subjects of the following poems. You can find trail guides to download and more information about walking and hiking on our conserved lands at MonadnockConservancy.org

Monadnock Conservancy
Featured Properties

①   **John and Rosemarie Calhoun Family Forest, Gilsum**

②   **Whittemore Island, Thorndike Pond, Jaffrey**

③   **Cunningham Pond Conservation Area, Peterborough**

④   **Chamberlain Conservation Area, Fitzwilliam**

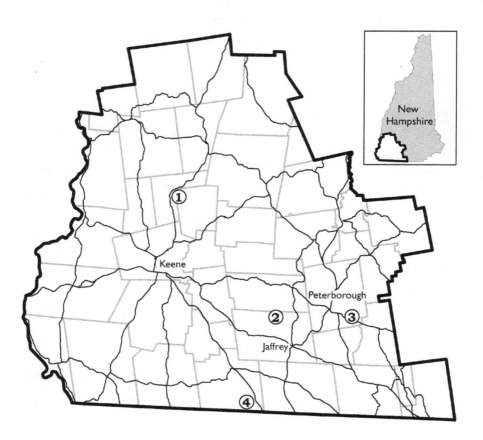

John and Rosemarie Calhoun Family Forest
Gilsum, New Hampshire

Forester John Calhoun and his wife, Rosemarie, owned and managed
this property for half a century. The five Calhoun children have fond
memories of cutting firewood, picnics at Porcupine Falls, and swimming
in White Brook. They chose to donate the 335-acre property to the
Monadnock Conservancy in 2011 to honor their parents' legacy, ensuring
sound stewardship of their family's land forever. An easy trail through
the woods, rich with mosses and ferns, follows the brook and culminates
at a bridge—a wonderful spot from which to enjoy "Porky Falls."

Calhoun Family Forest I: Gilsum, NH
by Rodger Martin

Abandon the pavement and parking of Route 10,
after marveling at the great vault
of the arched, granite bridge lording
century-and-a-half over the roaring Ashuelot,
slide onto the squish of March mud ruts,
frosting on a frozen base hard as granite,
and walk upward alongside White Brook
yet to infuse itself with the tannins of this land.
Always upward, follow a nuthatch's arcing flight,
its hungry call, upward to a hard-crafted stone stairway
and its green rock cap where children and grandchildren
rushed for their midnight summers' dreamings.

Upward to Porcupine Falls, spring melt spurting
through a thin split in the rock. Sit awhile, think
on the child you once were, the person you have lost.
Let that child frolic a bit in the glen, and then,
rested, walk with your memory all the way down.

Calhoun Family Forest II—Almost a Sonnet
by Rodger Martin

After the line of late day squalls, a close,
blue breeze skits between crust lichen and moss-
covered limbs. It echoes dappled sunlight
afoot on duff untouched for generations.
Elsewhere too, the sanctity of lost song
tugs at the eaves of crowned oak and maple.
And what of the feldspar, garnet, beryl,
and smoky quartz? Crystals withdrawn on sites
which beget lanes and highways to transport them
to skylines, those grand, monumental shots
to nothingness. Let the mica remain,
let it glitter among the tourmaline—
faceted testimonials to what
we're not—predating all we've ever known.

White Brook's "Porky Falls" by Katrina Farmer

Calhoun Family Forest III: The Legends
by Rodger Martin

A fecund, lunar vapor stirs the nostrils
as the trail winds its way to Skull Rock:
Keeper of Stones,
Guardian of Granite Outcroppings.
It marks each traveler
approaching its iridescent broomfork,
"Is this one worthy?"
And for each who passes,
the story door opens.

1.

An azalea sphinx flutters across stone steps
to the bridge. It alights on the other side,
contemplates the flame of the sun.
Is this the innocent heal-all?

2.

A swift courses acrobatically through timbers,
locked in its search for sustenance.
Each sudden twist a possibility,
each a future somewhere else.

3.

In a dank hollow beneath the ledges,
generations of quills wait
for the boy hiding from his seekers.
A brother earns his name.

4.

A man and his hiking stick return
after wintering with his daughter
on the tidal flats of Virginia. Each day
finds him walking with memory of her mother.

5.

One warbling vireo gabs gossip
with a black-throated green warbler—
cousins in tenacity and woodland chatter
carried from before the Abenaki.

6.

A road led to Sullivan in the age when travelers
did not concern themselves with comfort, a track
children skied from hilltop to base not concerned
with anyone or thing coming the other way.

7.

Such a road could lead to Switzerland's
solstice moon setting an alpine meadow aglow,
where the blue shadow of an angel
suggests the perfect spruce for Christmas.

8.

Parked aside a logging trail in the older growth,
a green jeep waits on a forester and small boy
learning to mark trees. Instead, the boy learns
a different compass and true north.

9.

Above the falls, behind the ledge, five islands
among the wood stubbled rivulets become stardust
for five children. Each island, a tiny spiral galaxy.
Each galaxy, a stepping stone to their expanding universe.

Whittemore Island
Jaffrey, New Hampshire

The 5.4-acre Whittemore Island, in the center of Thorndike Pond, was saved from resort development by the Whittemore family in the middle of the 20th century. The island, now owned by the Monadnock Conservancy, is accessible by boat in the summer—a time when loons and blueberries can often be found. A small network of trails offers a destination spot for paddlers and boaters looking for a peaceful place to enjoy.

Poems for Whittemore Island, Thorndike Pond, Jaffrey, NH, June 2021

For the Horizons
by Alice B. Fogel

At the boundary of lake and land the sand's
    carved in fine lines and even clouds
        ikat, tricked into parallel
ripples submerged in the water.
    Mosses and bowed branches tint
        the shallows a pallid
muddy green. Trees step down to the shore
    and keep on pressing
        their bodies deeper
into the muck below—and meanwhile
    this pulse won't stop wavering against
        the earth, making
its small sounds
    just beneath an overhanging ground.
        An island
is an old nest woven into wet-winded boughs
    that dress its edge in mulched debris—
        fungi and larvae in bloom between
dead twigs and leaves—all stages at once
    of becoming and dying and time.
        There are no
horizons that don't change or can't change

us—depending
        on when and where we stand
in relation to them
        and to erosion and roots,
                the rains and the droughts—
our boots skimming one surface, our boats
        drawn up for now out of the pond,
                our widening
circles spinning from the weighted center
        all the way out and beyond—

For the Ground
by Alice B. Fogel

With the great angles of the mountain just beyond the horizon,
the height of the white pines and hemlocks bearing sky,

and the circle of land around the lakeside's distance,
it's the spring ground I'm drawn to peer at most: its moss-muted

echo of new maple leaves' green, its deep golden lichen a fake
fox fur, the fallen and dried cones and catkins sprinkling

soil into a texture akin to the flakes of bark on trunks,
or like the small criss-crossings of waves that moat the shores.

Here at my feet sink all the old beech's cool shades
of browns and tans and grays as last year's leaves age into earth

and fresh sprouts arise bright and lean into the tripletted forms
of trillium, the starbursts of sweet woodruff, red seeds

dropped and strewn and growing through blown-down branches:
all the piled plenty of loss left of the past,

all the tiniest hints and most insistent hedged bets of the future.

For What the Water Defines
by Alice B. Fogel

Backlit and limited by the lake, this island woods' range shifts
the context of woods: dark trunks
of varying angles and widths and bends don't blend

but stand clear of each other, all their forms and more—
like the curved hillocks and dips of ground—
defined in bright contour by the lake and its light.

This is what water does to our sight on the island:
It changes how we see the space and shape of everything:

The way the sky seems blue and white because of the lake
and not the other way around. The way the contrasting

limbs and hedges hang over water and air, always at an edge.
Even the earth leans over its own eaves.

It's the water's dimensions between island and the land
across from it that defines the water, and the island, and the land:

Where a log that's come to rest partly in the pond
becomes a new pier for growth. Where raised roots hold tight
or let go of boulders they've grown around.

The difference between the bleached tan pulp of the fallen half
of a pine and the deeper moist brown of the half
left standing. The ragged piece of sky that part pierces.

How the paler leaves point a path through undergrowth. How
sunlight and shade alternate on the forest floor.

Pauses between the seven ladyslippers. Between the visible
lines of branches, needles, and smoothed domes of stone. Lees
and peaks of waves, blinking dark and light.

The difference between the bird drifting toward the canopy
on the opposite shore and the bird dipping its wings into shallows.
Between when I remember the island and when I was there.

Cunningham Pond Conservation Area
Peterborough, New Hampshire

A group of Peterborough residents, calling themselves the Cunningham
Pond Preservation Alliance, sought the Monadnock Conservancy's
help to save this property after three building lots on the east shore
were subdivided and sold. After a major community-based fundraising
campaign, the Conservancy purchased the property in 2019, protecting
forever 99 acres, including a half mile of shoreline and nearly a mile
of scenic frontage on Route 101. New trails connect visitors to wood-
lands, a hilltop field, sweeping views of Pack Monadnock and Temple
Mountain, and an old carriage road at the water's edge.

Renewal
Ann B. Day

Last week in the gray light of a late April dawn
I walked a narrow path through the damp woods.
Bare, black branches of hardwood shrubs and trees
paled as fog drifted between ash, birch and maple.
In the mist, I saw the silhouette of a crow on top
of a butternut tree. It lifted off and, silently
with feather fanned, it slid away into the fog.
fading black to gray to gone.

Again, I walk the path on an early May morning.
The rising sun beams through trees and warms
the soil. Sugar maples glow with tiny green foliage
spilling from their pods. Blood root, spring beauties,
trout lilies are blooming. White birches are bursting
with yellow and young crows cackle in their nests.

Over Cunningham Pond
by Ann B. Day

Slow floating high above Cunningham Pond, its dark
primaries spread to catch the westerly wind, it turns,
wavers, tips, turns again in ever widening circles up
and up against cloud-dotted blue.

Head tips, right, left, black eyes search where brown
grass meets shrubs and the last bit of lingering snow
while tall white pines frame the field like elder states-
men observing activity in the meadow.

Field mice venture out to search for seed. The hawk,
now a dot in the sky, circles as it watches the mice below
watching for something larger. The afternoon sun catches
the red in the hawk's tail.

On the ground a young groundhog nibbles on fresh grass.
The red-tail sees it, turns downward, eyes fixed on its prey
with its talons stretched forward, It screeches as it streaks
downward toward the field.

In seconds it lands in grassy brush at edge of the field.
After a moment of silence, the red-tail rises up, wings
pumping, limp groundhog in its claws, it flies east over
the pond to the pine forest on Pack Monadnock.

Beech Leaves
by Ann B. Day

Why do the pale, bronze leaves
of beech betray the legacy of fall
by holding fast to stubborn twigs
beyond the time of autumn's call?

Through winter winds and storms
they cling reluctant to let go
until the gentle nudge of spring
drops them awash in melting snow.

I see them in the winter woods,
a yellow patch in barren trees, their
parchment curls are clustered near
and quiver in the cold north breeze.

Perhaps, like them, I cling too much
to seasons past and seasons seen,
for spring will come with burst of buds
to fill a waiting world with green.

Beech leaves by Jackson Farmer

Chamberlain Conservation Area
Fitzwilliam, New Hampshire

The plan was for a house on this 77-acre property on Sip Pond. But when his wife passed, Craig Chamberlain decided against it, thinking land conservation was a better option to honor her. Since 2018, the Monadnock Conservancy has welcomed the public. It's easy to get to the scenic point, thanks to the Cheshire Rail Trail that borders the property and a new accessible trail with views of Mount Monadnock.

I got an assignment/challenge to write a poem about The Chamberlain lot on the south end of Sip Pond in Fitzwilliam. I could have, and maybe should have written the poem about the Chamberlain family. It was by their generously that made it possible for Monadnock Conservancy to buy the organization's first piece of land. Somehow the poem took a different direction. My wife, Beth, and I visited the land one cold and windy February day. We walked out on the ice and over the rocks just to get a feel for the place. Following this, there was no immediate inspiration. About 3 weeks after visiting the land though, I was headed to Sunapee to ski. All of a sudden, while driving, I got the idea about the giant's hand. And how that land came to be! I pulled the car over and wrote it down. And the ski day was very satisfying.

—Swift Corwin 3/17/21

Sip Pond Giant
by Swift Corwin

Who remembers when the great giant ran up from Massachusetts
Way before it was Massachusetts
And fell smack on his back
Just short of Monadnock?

Maybe it was even before the glacier left behind the big hole making Sip Pond in what would someday become Fitzwilliam, New Hampshire. Now, all that is left to show is an upturned hand and a craggy finger pointed north, straight to that mountain.

People here can't remember.
Some don't even think of it. But, there is talk.
Nothing conclusive has come of it.

It has been so long since the fall,
that from the surrounding bog, where his rocky hand remains,
grows a bed of blueberries, leatherleaf, black spruce, and larch.
It's a soft resting place, that south shore of the pond.

Mink, otter, and bobcat mince over its granite boulder wrist
as if it belonged to them.
They might be chasing mice and red squirrels
fattening themselves on pine seeds.
While beaver feast on red maple an birch saplings
at the edges by the blueberries in the rocks.

And the finger always keeps pointing north into New Hampshire.

As they walk to the north on the point,
people visiting might not even notice.
They are on an upturned hand!

But, then they might.

A while back, folks were so fascinated to look at the point
that they decided to build a cabin on the mucky, adjacent west shore.
Just to get the closest look.
Judging from the tracks across the ice, the cabin is still popular.
Windows have even been broken to improve the view.

Somehow the New Hampshire forest,
Being the New Hampshire forest,
Has decided to make that rocky hand its own.
White pines have grown in rocky crags and crevices,
From wrist to fingertip.

At the end of the once...soft fingertip.
A pine has an eagle-claw grip holding the tree fast to rock.

The wind always blows, hard, from the northwest.
The tree is a weather-worn creation,
But these claw roots have grown heavy.
And they don't look like they will be giving up anytime soon.

This pine will stand a Sip Pond beacon for years to come.

Sometime in the future,
more may be known about the giant.
People around here find stuff like this out.

They always do.

Kennebec Estuary Land Trust

Bath, ME

The Kennebec Estuary Land Trust is committed to conserving land and wildlife habitat of the Lower Kennebec and Sheepscot River estuaries. We are a volunteer-driven, donor-supported organization serving the communities of Arrowsic, Bath, Bowdoinham, Dresden, West Bath, Georgetown, Richmond, Westport Island and Woolwich.

An estuary is a partially enclosed body of water along the coast where freshwater from rivers and streams meet and mix with salt water from the ocean. Estuaries and the lands surrounding them are places of transition from land to sea, providing important refuge for wildlife to feed, roam, and thrive. The Kennebec River contributes an average of six billion gallons of water to the Gulf of Maine per day, making its influence on the state's water quality and overall ecological health significant. KELT maintains twelve preserves for public enjoyment and has protected 4,100+ acres of land since our founding in 1989. Learn more by visiting www.kennebecestuary.org or calling (207) 442-8400.

-Red Rose Preserve-Jeri Theriault
-Bonyun Preserve-David Crews
-Green Point Preserve-Mike Bove
-Higgins Mountain Preserve-Robert Carr
-Lilly Pond Community Forest-Julian Wise
-Merrymeeting Fields Preserve-Dawn Potter

Red Rose Preserve

listening to the forest
by Jeri Theriault

I walk the Gully Trail   the Farm Road Loop
taking i-phone pictures of white pine & paper birch
—my growing-up-Maine habitat.

at the top of the trail   I sit on a mossy stump
to write in my journal made of pulpwood
from the kind of trees my grandfather logged

in the north woods. I hear birds
& my own breath   not the trees' sun-stretch
root-reach   whatever they say   uncluttered

& slow. roots twined by fungi   underground
symbiosis & above-ground   volatile organic
compounds—I know they keep a party-line

for vital news   as when the Sitka willows
battled pests by telegraphing warnings to kin
miles away—CATERPILLARS COMING. STOP.

RELEASE TOXINS. STOP. what are the trees
saying now? I want them to see me—stranger
not enemy. clumsy in my city shoes

skin wrapped snug from sun & soil   I head back
to the parking lot   pine-scent   twig-crunch
my solitary brain   numb to arboreal knowing.

in the shadow of tallness
by Jeri Theriault

we mostly walk past
mosses   eyes drawn

by swaying pines
& Cardinals. but here

these low-slung stars
overlooked

underseen   weave
lush green

out of the wind's fray
a thriving tiny sonnet

this tender turn
moss   a counterpane

a galaxy   weaving
earth & air.

wanting blue
by Jeri Theriault

Eastern white pines stretch into the sky-dome
creatures of updraft & drift   alive with wind
& want. beings of earth   they are ambassadors
to air   embracing blue the way their roots
hold microbes & worms   warm
in the wintering soil. we have forgotten
their worth & silent strength   their slow time
as we look up—the way we always do—craving
that pine   that very blue for our own.

Red Rose Preserve by Kennebec Estuary Land Trust

Bonyun Preserve

This past fall, I found placement to work at an organic farm along the coast of Maine in a little town called Phippsburg. It was Rachel Carson's third book in her trilogy on the seas that brought me here, and I was immediately drawn—as so many are—to the geology of the Maine coast. Here, bedrock and evergreen forest stretch all the way down to much of the shore line. The glacial history has both carved a rugged mountain terrain and flooded much of the coast where, at the edge of the sea, one can find some incredible estuary ecosystems. An estuary is an example of an ecotone—a region of transition between biological communities—where saltwater from the sea mixes with freshwater from the river to generate a complex ecosystem in flux. The below poem is part of a larger sequence for the Kennebec Estuary Land Trust titled "Kennebec River," though this particular visit to Bonyun Preserve on Westport Island—what is Abenaki ancestral land—occurred on a quiet morning in October.

--David Crews, Nov. 2020

Bonyun Preserve
by David Crews

I walk the wooded trail down to the estuary, a return

big trees loom—white pine, hemlock, balsam fir

they will follow the descent of the land, where the tides
move

ebb and flow

the water's pull upon rock, root

wind in the pines

wind in the pines

pine wind

pine song

Green Point Preserve

Green Point Preserve, West Bath
by Mike Bove

Raven, nuthatch, woodpecker:
there are voices in the woods.
Other sounds, too, at the water where
seaweed waves with the tide.
If you think about it, and you do,
there's no way to say where
your footsteps end and the land begins,
so you need to take care, the birds
remind you, take good care because
though you're alone,
you're not the only one here.

Green Point Preserve by Kennebec Estuary Land Trust

Considering the Timeline, Green Point Preserve
by Mike Bove

1.

The beginning of the timeline states
the Abenaki stewarded the region
prior to white settlement.
What if:
Beginnings are arbitrary.
The land did not require settling.

2.

Timelines are wrong to suggest
the present is a destination
we've arrived at.

3.

We like the way this land accepts
our footsteps.
We like the moss and spruce, the rocks
that wall the waves.
We like the way this land remembers
our children running the path,
the way it remembers us as children.
We like the parallel memories
of the Abenaki
watching their children.

4.

Everyone knows beginnings
and endings are the same.

Walking With My Sons at Green Point
by Mike Bove

Small trees aspire upward.
Like children.
Like my boys who
walk here and touch all they can:
shawls of moss on a pine,
minty lichen blooms
on a half-buried boulder.
When they reach the point
they scramble for rock shards
and pebbles, hurling them
as far as they can into water,
competing for length.
I want to tell them to watch
the ripples that pulse outward
from each splash.
I want to give them a metaphor
for the way small choices
reach toward forever.
I don't say anything.
They'll know it when
they're grown, tall
like trees, some later day
when they're not
trying to outdo each other
in distance.

Higgins Mountain Preserve

Higgins Mountain Without My Father
by Robert Carr

I've come to *Lichen*
Loop to find quiet
in the cracks of my face.
Everything about this
mountain, split.
Ageless granite, wedged
apart by ice.
Stone, crowned
by deep green pillows,
boulders wrapped
in blankets of *British*
Soldier. At the summit
I find deer scat
on a bed of needle.
I am tired.
The buck, somewhere
hidden in scrub
brush. I touch
the season of ground
cover, lichen and moss,
the final rift
of fathers and their sons.

Something Pretty
by Robert Carr

Skin cools through worn jeans.

I sit on a stone cairn,
where Land Trust signage

warns: *Leave All Rocks
Exactly Where You Found Them.*

I roll fungi between fingers,
mica chips lose sparkle
in my pocket, I toss

a skimming stone across a bed
of oak leaves. Tragic, human,

I can't touch a place
without taking something pretty.

Higgins Mountain Preserve by Kennebec Estuary Land Trust

Georgetown Island
by Robert Carr

An oak and I have stumbled
on the mountain –
broken bark and bloodied shins.
I lean on the nurse
tree, a thick pitch pine.

She shines graffito shades
of green. I roll fungus,
oddly familiar,
in my scuffed palm. A phone-app
names the unfamiliar:

Cladonia: food source
for the caribou, last seen
in Maine on the saddle of Katahdin,
a hundred years ago.

Harvested and sold as fake trees
for model train displays.

That's it, why this feels
like childhood!

Artificial landscapes – bubbling
lights, asbestos snow, tinsel
on spruce branches, the dyed fare
of vanquished caribou.

I'm quieted by memories –
electric trains, the Lionel Line,
circling Christmas trees.

Injured on this mountain,
I negotiate my place
in an ocean wind of highways
down below, the pencil
yellow loads on logging trucks,
the screaming crow.

Lilly Pond Community Forest

Lilly Pond
by Jullian Wise

When searching for Lilly Pond
I found myself lost
in unfamiliar territory.

Before feeling lost, however,
I embarked on a grand quest with a sense of desire
and a thirst for treasure.

At the fork between Grandpa's Trail and Lilly Pond Trail
past the occasional rusted piece of iron
around the descending bend
into a sudden division between coniferous on my left
and deciduous on my right

I paused within the chasm
and glared up at the full coverage of hardy evergreens
that took precedence over the last of the oak and maple leaves.

I allowed myself to pause, just for a moment.
Pause and wonder
what would be lost without these woods?

Shelter for the migratory birds who visit Maine's rocky coast;
home for the native species of the region;
a peaceful getaway for human inhabitants
who can dive into instant adventure within the trees
just as I had.

What would be lost? I ask
if the seas rise
or the brush burns
or the animals cannot live any longer
as drought denies their food.

Would the ship builders keep building?
Would the walkers keep walking?
Would the lobstermen keep harvesting?
Would the farmers keep farming?
All as they had before?

Lilly Pond by Kennebec Estuary Land Trust

Merrymeeting Fields Preserve

Pandemic Field Notes
by Dawn Potter

The ticks are waking up, or so I've heard.
I should visit them,
but it turns out I've forgotten
how to drive to new places.

* * *

I pore over the map, that mournful record
of time, old riverine choked in a net of asphalt.
Where is my heavenly sign, assuring me
"This is where you are"?

* * *

In 1791 a man invented a tame vision of the Kennebec
butting into the head of Merrymeeting Bay.
"Navigable for small Vessells," his drawing promised.
As if: "The wild is no trouble at all."

* * *

My terror of travel is not fake.
I say this to make myself feel better because
in 1791 I would not be here. I would still be
in Poland eating cabbage. Oppression be damned.

* * *

Before maps there were paths.
Before paths there were other paths.
Always, a beast's feet threading a kill zone.
Still, water wins in the end.

* * *

For twenty-five years I lived next to a vernal
pool in a forest. Lots of frogs, but the mud stayed put.
So what's the deal with these thrashing river mouths,
tearing up their beds like myth-monsters?

* * *

Aha! you crow.
So you *did* travel!
Yes, but I kicked and screamed
the whole way.

* * *

Dear armchair traveler, dear
couch potato, what is a voyage?
I lie on my back in the wet dead bracken and stare up
into the leafless maples. Probably a tick is crawling on me.

* * *

One thing I do know:
paddling a tidal river is hard.
I may never do it again,
unless I get homesick for monsters.

Merrymeeting Fields Preserve by Kennebec Estuary Land Trust

 NEW ENGLAND **FORESTRY** FOUNDATION

New England Forestry Foundation

Littleton, MA

A hike through a New Hampshire forest in the fall; a Vermont barn made from locally milled trees; and the clear, clean waters of a Maine river—these are just a few of the many gifts that New England's forests offer. Across the region, forests provide timber for construction, local jobs, wildlife habitat, clean air and water, and recreational opportunities. These benefits support a vibrant and thriving region, and New England Forestry Foundation (NEFF) works to protect them for future generations. Founded in 1944, NEFF pursues innovative programs to advance conservation, sustainable forestry, and forest-related climate solutions throughout New England. In partnership with land owners, NEFF has conserved more than 1.1 million acres of forest, including one out of every three acres of forestland protected in New England since 1999. This makes NEFF the nation's third largest land trust.

-Niantic River Headwaters-Lori Landau
-Lincoln Davis Forest-bg Thurston

New England Forestry Foundation

New England Forestry Foundation (NEFF) is the only nonprofit organization in New England that specializes in both the continuous improvement of the practice of forest management and the conservation of working forests, a crucial and beautiful feature of the region's landscape.

During NEFF's more than 75 years of history, in-house experts have created a forest management approach called Exemplary Forestry; it prioritizes forests' long-term health and outlines the highest standards of sustainability currently available to the region's forest owners. In addition to protecting forests and their ecosystem services, Exemplary Forestry is designed to accomplish three goals: enhance the role forests can play to mitigate climate change, improve wildlife habitat, and grow and harvest more of the wood forests are capable of producing sustainably.

Exemplary Forestry has become a key component of NEFF's major initiative to mitigate climate change, the Forest-to-Cities Climate Challenge, and Exemplary Forestry is also now practiced on all of NEFF's more than 150 Community Forests—Lincoln Davis Memorial Forest and Niantic River Headwaters Community Forest included.

Everyone at NEFF hopes visitors to these two special places and NEFF's other Community Forests will have a chance to see that high-quality forest management is compatible with forests' many values, including serving as a source of inspiration. NEFF's Community Forests include places of great scenic beauty, like the Berry Pasture Trail described in bg Thurston's poem of the same name, the shore of Squam Lake as seen from NEFF's Chamberlain Reynolds Memorial Forest, and the Bill Merrill Mountain summit on Merrill Mountain Community Forest. They also include plainer woods that still provide opportunities for visitors to contemplate the growth, death, decay, and rebirth of the forest.

Photo: A hiker explores Niantic River Headwaters Community Forest by Tinsley Hunsdorfer (lower right)

Photo: Visitors gather for a guided walk of Niantic River Headwaters Community Forest that NEFF held to celebrate the completion of the forestland's first phase of conservation by Carson Hauck (above)

A River on Its Way to the Bay

In 2019, NEFF completed conservation of 200 acres of critical habitat at its Niantic River Headwaters Community Forest in East Lyme, CT. This project was undertaken in two phases: NEFF first conserved 166 acres of the forest in 2017, and then protected an adjacent 34-acre parcel two years later.

Located about five miles from Niantic Bay—into which the Niantic River flows—and the Connecticut coastline, the Niantic River Headwaters Community Forest is well worth seeing. Visitors can get a look at the Niantic River's early stages, as well as the forest's most dramatic feature, a rocky ridge line. The property also has an established system of trails, and members of the public are welcome to head out for a walk and explore this beautiful and ecologically important forestland.

Home to diverse wildlife, plant communities, wetland resources, and topography, the Niantic River Headwaters Community Forest is part of a larger 2,200-acre forest block in East Lyme and Waterford. This significant area of forested corridor is comprised of approximately twenty parcels, mostly privately owned. The conservation of Niantic River Headwaters Community Forest ensures that water flowing from a portion of the headwaters will continue to be filtered by the forest and natural wetland habitat, thereby helping to maintain water quality in the river's estuary.

The Niantic River Headwaters marks NEFF's fourth Community Forest in Connecticut, and its close ties to salt water also make the property stand out in the NEFF Community Forest network. Only three NEFF properties have salt water frontage: Holmes Stream Community Forest in Whiting, ME; Arnold Family Forest in Freeport, ME; and Nelson Memorial Forest in Marshfield, MA. NEFF's new Frenchman Bay Community Forest in Hancock, ME has a more Niantic-like setup, meaning they both have a short and direct connection to salt water: a stream that runs through the Frenchman property flows into the saltwater Kilkenny Cove about two miles from NEFF's property line.

These points where land transitions to sea make for striking destinations that bustle with wildlife—and serve as a fascinating introduction to NEFF's Community Forests.

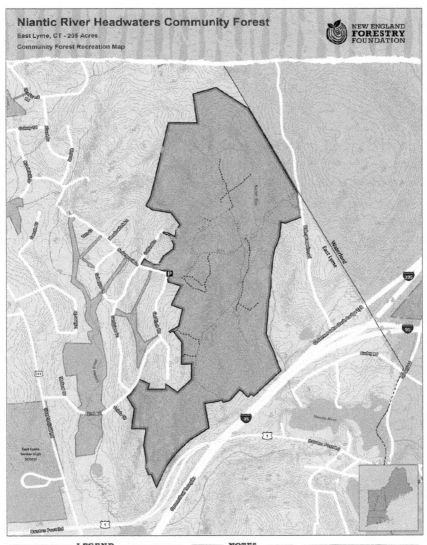

Niantic River Headwaters Community Forest
East Lyme, CT - 205 Acres
Community Forest Recreation Map

NEW ENGLAND
FORESTRY
FOUNDATION

LEGEND

NEFF Land	- - - Maintained Trails
Other Protected Open Space	- - - Unmaintained Trails
P Roadside Parking	Open Water
Contours	Wetlands
Town boundary	Streams

NOTES

Refer to the NEFF website for Community Forest recreation guidelines and regulations.

Maintained trail distances are shown in miles.
Contour interval is 5 ft.

Credits: ESRI 'Terrain Base' map service

Date 4/6/2018

0   300   600   1,200
Feet

Niantic River Headwater

At the tail end of the Pandemic amidst enormous global and personal losses, I visited the New England Forestry Foundation as a poetry ambassador for a project called Writing the Land. I drew on my meditation practice, eastern philosophy, and eco-somatic work to explore my deep interest in a felt-sense relationship between human nature, and nature itself. I hoped my poems would be a visceral reminder of how our survival as a species is mutually dependent with that of the planet. I wanted to use poetry as a vehicle for activism, to create both beauty and awareness for forest conservation work and in doing so, be part of dreaming a sustainable future. These poems were written in response to my time among the area's trees, grasses, birds, waters, diverse array of plants, animals, and wildlife. May they speak for the next generations who rely on us to care for this fragile land we call home.

—Lori Landau 6/28/21

Space Between
by Lori Landau

Nothing more than wren singing,

nothing less.
in thicket of trees.
                me

drinking the sound.

Ode to Robin
(*State Bird of Connecticut*)
by Lori Landau

teach me
how to have wings
to soar over moss and stone
see the river whole
fly forward into light
disturbing nothing but air.

Some Things Cannot be Stolen
by Lori Landau

Green cordgrass slows
the banks of
long-neck waters
at the edge of trails,
ancestral home
to the Nehantic.

One third of these Wetlands stolen.
Settlers swindled the sacred stone
tore peace from the pines
plundered quarries, splintered trees.

Oak resisted
dug roots.
Nourished itself
in the brackish tide.

I traveled here from a distance
to witness resilience
be still with my losses

learn from this old tree

how to plant in shattered soil
and begin again.

Cooperative Conservation at Lincoln Davis Memorial Forest

When NEFF was founded, the practice of private organizations protecting land through ownership was largely untried in the United States. In honor of NEFF's 75th anniversary, staff members in 2019 took an in-depth look at NEFF's first forest, the Lincoln Davis Memorial Forest of 1945, to see what the conservation process looked like in those days.

This beautiful, mountainous New Hampshire forestland has come to exemplify the outsize ecosystem impact protected land can have when it's conserved collaboratively and with an eye to the wider landscape. Lincoln Davis is partially surrounded by a series of contiguous protected forestlands, with additional conserved land nearby.

Like many of NEFF's forests, Lincoln Davis sustains wildlife habitat, provides recreation opportunities, and locks away carbon every year—helping to hold damaging climate change at bay. Each year, the trees of the forest turn sunlight, water, and carbon dioxide from the air into wood. NEFF's Exemplary Forestry approach helps ensure that carbon sequestration and storage in the forest is maintained at high levels. Since 1945, the amount of carbon stored in Lincoln Davis' trees has increased by more than 61,000 metric tons, the same amount as would be emitted by burning 6.9 million gallons of gasoline. During this same time period, NEFF harvested 33,665 tons of wood, material that helped reduce emissions by being used to build homes in place of fossil-fuel intensive materials like steel and concrete. Exemplary Forestry helps forestlands help all living things, wildlife included, avoid the worst of climate change.

Lincoln Davis helps wildlife more directly too. Much of New England's remaining private forestland—particularly in the southern portion of the region—has been carved into parcels that are too small to singlehandedly support the full suite of native wildlife. Roads and houses that proliferate in this fragmented landscape can cut animals off from reproductive partners and force them into degraded habitat as they seek food and shelter. By strategically protecting contiguous land parcels that connect to important habitat, New Englanders can give wild animals safe passage to the resources they need to thrive—and, for species more prone to wandering, simply provide them with enough space.

Camilla Lockwood, one of four landowners who have granted conservation easements to NEFF on parcels around Lincoln Davis Memorial Forest, enjoys tracking the conservation status of nearby parcels to "see new green squares lining up like puzzle pieces."

"There's a lot of land around here, but that doesn't do big critters any good if they can't get from one place to another," Camilla said. "They need large, unrestricted areas to roam, and I'm excited that my land is helping to fill in some gaps."

Not only do contiguous pieces of well-managed forestland give wild animals stretches of uninterrupted habitat, but they also do a better job of protecting headwaters for clean water downstream. And more opportunities for long-distance hiking trails don't hurt, either.

One such trail currently crosses Lincoln Davis Memorial Forest and its surrounding NEFF conservation easements in the Temple Mountain area of south-central New Hampshire; called the Wapack Trail, this popular hikers' route opened in 1923 and runs north-south for 21 miles from Mount Watatic in Ashburnham, MA, to North Pack Monadnock in Greenfield, NH.

The Steady Growth of NEFF's First Forest and Temple Mountain Easements

NEFF first established a presence on Temple Mountain in 1945 when Dr. Lincoln Davis deeded a 607-acre parcel to NEFF that became the Lincoln Davis Memorial Forest. Dr. Davis was a surgeon at Massachusetts General Hospital, and in the 1920s and 1930s, often traveled to this well-loved woodland to enjoy time with his family.

Thomas Cabot and Virginia Wellington Cabot then gave NEFF an adjoining 176 acres in 1964 that include the crest of Temple Mountain. Tom Cabot was a dedicated conservationist who served as a member of the NEFF corporation and as president of the Appalachian Mountain Club, and who had a long-running attachment to Temple Mountain. He and his wife were outdoor enthusiasts who summered there for years, and a two-mile section of the Wapack Trail is now known as the Cabot Skyline in honor of his donation of a trail easement and to recognize him as "a lifelong friend of the Wapack Trail."

Photo: The view-complete with soaring Turkey Vulture-from the Wapack Trail near NEFF's Lincoln Davis Memorial Forest (above)

Photo: The popular 21-mile Wapack Trail crosses Lincoln Davis Memorial Forest and its surrounding NEFF conservation easements; the Wapack also directly intersects with Lincoln Davis' Berry Pasture Trail (previous page)

~Both photos by Tinsley Hunsdorfer~

Lincoln Davis Memorial Forest's final expansion occurred in 1985 when Clarissa Morse gave 146 acres in memory of her husband, Lovett Morse; the property's full name was thereafter changed to Lincoln Davis-Cabot-Morse Memorial Forest, though "Lincoln Davis" is still used as shorthand.

As NEFF's oldest forest, Lincoln Davis has proven to be a key testing ground for Exemplary Forestry. NEFF's 1998 Foundation Forests report summarizes the property's status at the time:

"A great deal of marketable timber has been cut from the Lincoln Davis property on a sustainable basis and today the forest has more standing timber, in far better health, than on the day Dr. Davis deeded it to NEFF. A variety of forest management activities has improved habitat for many species of wildlife."

This progress was made possible by the hard work of NEFF foresters assigned to the Monadnock Region, starting with Milt Attridge, NEFF's first full-time forester and later chief forester. The forest continues to thrive thanks to NEFF's current land stewardship staff and New England Forestry Consultants foresters Dan Reed and Dennis McKenney.

The number of NEFF-protected acres on Temple Mountain began to grow once more in the late 1990s when some of the landowners near Lincoln Davis looked into ways to protect their forestland without selling it. After speaking with a NEFF land protection staff member about her options, Camilla Lockwood became the first neighbor to take the conservation easement plunge. She decided to place easements on two parcels in 1998 and turned to NEFF as the best organization to hold them.

The wildlife corridor formed by Camilla's easements and the Lincoln Davis-Cabot-Morse Memorial Forest expanded in 2000 and 2001, when the Karl family, PJ and Tina O'Rourke, and the Cabot New Hampshire Land Trust each completed adjacent NEFF easements. This brought the total number of contiguous Temple Mountain acres protected by NEFF to 1,497, and the total length of Wapack Trail on NEFF-protected lands to well over a mile—not a bad legacy for NEFF's first forest, and a collective conservation achievement to be proud of.

Lincoln Davis-Cabot-Morse Memorial Forest and Surrounding Easements

Sharon & Temple, NH   929 Total NEFF Community Forest Acres   568 Total NEFF Conservation Easement Acres

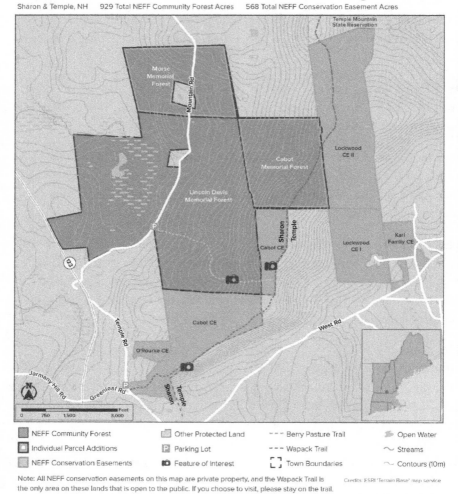

■ NEFF Community Forest	▣ Other Protected Land	- - - Berry Pasture Trail	🐾 Open Water
◨ Individual Parcel Additions	🅿 Parking Lot	- - - Wapack Trail	〜 Streams
▦ NEFF Conservation Easements	🔾 Feature of Interest	⌐⌐ Town Boundaries	〜 Contours (10m)

Note: All NEFF conservation easements on this map are private property, and the Wapack Trail is the only area on these lands that is open to the public. If you choose to visit, please stay on the trail.   Credits: ESRI 'Terrain Base' map service

Conservation of NEFF's First Forest and Surrounding Lands Over Time

> *1923: Wapack Trail opens*
> *1945: Lincoln Davis Memorial Forest donated to NEFF*
> *1964: Cabot parcel added to Lincoln Davis*
> *1985: Morse parcel added to Lincoln Davis*
> *1998: Lockwood I easement completed, Lockwood II easement completed*
> *2000: Karl Family easement completed*
> *2001: Cabot easement completed, O'Rourke easement completed*

Lincoln Davis Memorial Forest

The Love of Pinecones
by bg Thurston
            for Sharon H.

Souvenir of the forest—
where every tree is its own
miracle. Symbol of rebirth,
resurrection, and immortality,

the cones we see scattered
in these woods are female.
The males, having given up
their pollen, disintegrate

then disappear—leaving
the mother cones laden
with seeds hidden beneath
rows of overlapping scales.

A perfect Fibonacci sequence,
each cone forms a sturdy
vessel, protecting its treasure
by closing tight in rain or cold.

Native Americans gathered
them for food and medicine,
burned them as incense to pacify
ghosts and banish nightmares.

Pinecones represented Venus,
the Roman Goddess of Love,
while Celts placed them under
their pillows as fertility charms.

Someday, when you find one
hidden inside a forgotten pocket,
remember where it came from
and the promise it still holds.

Berry Pasture Trail, Sharon, N.H.
by bg Thurston

Begin at the clearing where bluets
and buttercups bloom underfoot.

Find a narrow trail hidden by oak,
hemlock, white pine, and birch.

Mossy stones erupt along your path,
as blue blazes dot the uphill climb.

A sudden pond appears, reflecting
the interlaced hemlock branches.

Pause here to listen to the wood thrush
recite his vowel sounds under a sky

troubled by clusters of dark clouds
as rain begins to spatter treetops.

Keep going, though now your breath
has become much harder to catch.

Stand where blueberries once thrived,
look toward Monadnock's silhouette

and remember all those mountains
you hoped to climb someday.

Discover what you have dropped
as you turn to descend the summit—

a silver spinner ring you fingered
the whole of your worried last year.

No more than a cherished token
now returned to this wild universe.

A small 'O' that the moon will find
shining silent in the litter of leaves.

The Silent Poem of the Forest
by bg Thurston

A lone bronze soldier greets us,
holding his rifle and patriotic flag
in a tribute to another Civil War.

Uncertain of boundaries, we follow
the snow-covered road that divides
a stark wilderness of oak and fir

until we enter stillness, undercut
by a low thrum of far-away traffic.
No birds can be heard, no whisper

of wind, only the crunch of boots
threading through monochromatic trees
left from last year's logging. An upheaval

of wood settles into its new landscape
as we tread gently under widow-makers
and around trunks uprooted by storms.

Everywhere, stone walls remain
where hilly pastures once prevailed.
Through the pines, the sun burning—

as its molten glow sinks into the horizon
and though we know we should leave,
we persist despite frozen ink and fingers.

Before dusk, we return to the world
where history keeps on writing itself,
But these woods will call us back

to behold these places of furious beauty
where nature struggles to remind us—
here is where our true battles lie.

Mount Grace Land Conservation Trust

Athol, MA

Mount Grace Land Conservation Trust benefits the environment, the economy, and future generations by protecting significant agricultural, natural, and scenic lands and encouraging land stewardship in northern and central Massachusetts. The core strength of Mount Grace Land Conservation Trust is our focus on collaboration to achieve significant land protection projects while actively stewarding the conservation areas we own. Our effectiveness is a function of our creative, innovative approach and responsiveness to the diverse conservation ethics held by the landowners of our region.

-Dr. Allen Ross Memorial Canoe Launch-Michael Mauri
-Eagle Reserve Conservation Area-Candace R. Curran
-Sunset View Farm-Sharon A. Harmon

Community Conservation Program

The Community Conservation program is one that seeks to conserve land because it serves specific needs identified by the community. Working with teachers, veterans, retirees, hospitals, open space committees, and other stakeholders, Mount Grace plays a leadership role in translating local land needs into projects. We work to engage communities in strategic planning that empowers them to prioritize their goals for water, forestry, recreational, scenic, and wildlife habitat resources. As part of this process, we built coalitions to create accessible trails that can be enjoyed by all people.

Dr. Allen Ross Memorial Canoe Launch in Montague

In 1987, Dr. Allen Ross purchased 2.3 acres of pastoral fields, forest, and riparian habitat as a place to spend time in nature, to launch the family's kayaks and canoes, and to prevent development of the land. Allen was an avid canoe racer who regularly participated in local events like the River Rat Race in Athol.

"I spent countless summer days here – swimming, paddling up the river to the nearby islands, and relaxing in a hammock by the shady silver maples."
-Emma Ellsworth, daughter of Dr. Allen Ross

When Allen purchased the property, he was a member of the Mount Grace Board of Directors and active in the local conservation movement. In 2001 Ross worked with the Massachusetts Department of Conservation and Recreation (DCR) to place a Conservation Restriction on the land, ensuring the valuable riverside habitat was available for passive recreation and agriculture in perpetuity. It was around this time that Red Fire Farm entered into an agreement with Ross to farm along the front of the property, an agreement which remains active today.

Allen's children, Daniel Ross and Emma Ellsworth, are donating the parcel to Mount Grace so that their father's legacy will be honored by sharing his favorite place to enjoy the river with the whole community.

Photo: Dr. Allen Ross (right)

Poem by Michael Mauri. *Written with all due respect to any person possibly referenced or implied here and to any person not specifically mentioned or acknowledged, and in appreciation of the work of poet Lawrence Ferlinghetti, 1919 – 1921, whose words "I am signaling to you through the flames" inspired the opening lines of this poem, and to Rich Holschuh for sharing his insights on language and perception in his presentation Alosada Kpiwi - Let's Walk in the Woods: Finding Our Place Among All of Our Relations, presented on zoom (the internet) on June 15, 2021, and to all those who have worked and walked this land and worked to protect this land and will continue to do so to the extent they are able.*

Author's Statement: *A mindset of availing oneself to inspirations that may lead to the creation of a poem means being willing to go along in unforeseeable directions. My agreed-upon assignment for this poem was to be inspired by a certain place, a canoe launch to be soon created on the Connecticut River, though not yet existing. Standing there and looking across the wide river on a very cold late afternoon in November, I did not realize that my thoughts would be pulled strongly upriver, and then up another river, and then up yet another, to a mountain that still is and to people and visions that once were, to a place, also, which, through the culture, foresight and efforts of the Mount Grace Land Conservation Trust and the collaborations and affiliations it naturally attracts and fosters, has been protected. And though the old paths have been obscured and the rivers blocked along the way, the two places are still very much connected. And if at times a bald eagle floats over one, at other times a barred owl calls out at the other.*   *---M. Mauri, 7-1-2021*

It shall be kept free and open
by Michael Mauri

I am writing to you from across this river,
I am writing to you from across time.
And if there is no time, or if time is not real, then I am not writing
to you from across time or from across this river, but maybe from a
different season, a season when the oak was all aglow and the trees
somewhat shorter, though does it really come down to the inch?

A season when old Mr Harbindge still stood in the dooryard of his house
at the eastern toe of the mountain, beneath the steep and stony cliffy
slope, at the base of it, in the all-embracing *bree* and *lurious blithe* of its
braeful baern and *glith*, and he said I want you to cut all these pines,
but just the pines,
for only to these are we allergic, for they block the sun,
and they block the air we need, and they fill it with their pollen,
and the Mrs. is most allergic to them, come that time of year.

And he says cut these pines right to that ever-shifting, half-calculated,
Cartesian-concoculated, cross-zigged confabulation of invisible ambient
lines across the base of this mountain that serve as our boundary.

Cut, he says, right to the rusting, tilting wire fencing sagging ever inwards
and nearer.

Cut right to the freshly re-calibrated strands of twisted wire fence
repositioned every year when He who annually bookkeeps the inward-
reaching bushy scruffy scrubby growth of the pines comes around to
reset fence posts to the furthest conceivable inward heliotropic reach of
branch and needle and thus, alas, to our ever-accretioning reduction.

And thus are we somewhat vexed and ambiguated in the finding of the
true and deedful boundary as recorded in the registry of deeds in the
county courthouse at the county seat, which is the locality where such
perplexing and perpetuitous geometries are properly housed, and where
they are fastidiously logged in to bound books and numbered pages
and faithfully kept track of, he says, though the very county itself be
abolished.

And because of aforesaid you can even cut over that old fence a little, he says.

But now a hermit thrush sings in the woods, his nest near to where the house was, in the redolent pine of the air of the piney shady sunshiny redolent air, near the winding cicada heat of the sun-warmed gravel road, near the whirring mosquito shade of the cool maple grove, in the unending pines that can never be cut in their entirety.

And now a prairie warbler shimmers its ungrounded electric winding circuitry song of copper wiring and rewiring from the tall and un-mowed grasses, forbs, ferns, sedges and shrubs that once were hard-won fields of hay and pasture.

That once were logged-off, burned-off, stump-pulled, stone-picked, stone-hauled, stone-stacked, walked-over, scatter-sown, scythe-cut, raked-up, ricked-up, wagon-tracked, hoof-trodden, cow-called fields of hay and pasture.

And now that prairie warbler sings over across the gravelly dead-end road that did not used to be a dead-end road but now trickles out into a pine-needle footpath not far north of here.

And it sings over by the small dug pond that sits at day's end in the long, long shadow of this startling upright mountain being a mountain, come whatever may.

Well, they got cut, some of the pines did, anyway, and they even got cut again, at other times, but so, too, did the Mr and Mrs. themselves, and the loving house, even, disappearing into the mountain on one side and set back out onto the other side or just never even seen again - man, wife, house, dooryard and all.

And now there's not even a cellar hole to tell of it, or even a last lilac bush to bloom lately at the spot, or even a sign saying *here stood a homestead where a pleasant and honorable life was lived*, but why would there be such things? And can it be any more obvious that in thus-like manner all must go?

And now their loving spot is but a grassy swath and sward, and now it will remain such and even *shall* remain such, it is decreed, if that registry at the seat of that which is no longer a country in a true sense of the word keeps its enduring lock hold on each line, number, compass bearing and sentence, keeps its filed-away reference to each pipe, gun barrel and pin, stores its recorded mention of each purposefully-laid pile of stones and notable rotten stump, each momentous rusted axle and each torch-cut length of angle-iron sticking out of the ground.

And it shall be kept free and open.

Free and open for any buzzing pollinating wasps and bumble bees and twirling flapping butterflies and moths inexorably summoned by wild inflorescences, should any survive those actions we may yet still take or not take.

Free and open for any singing tumbling timber doodles fervidly sounding out their cold spring evenings' joy.

And for the hapless turtles shuffling along in strawberry season heat between pond, pines and fields, crisscrossing and scuffing in the sun-baked, long-gone dooryard at their hard-shell pace, marking with bent blade of grass and faint rescuffling of sand the wild dooryard where once we stood talking about pines, oh, pines.

And though true enough, all of these particulars are but part of the general case, not its entirety, and not necessarily even that which was observed earlier today by a clamorous indigo bunting impatiently peering from the top branches of the caterpillar-chewed, singular stout oak tree being an oak tree, between vanished house and persistent pond.

And may this unregisterable poem be a welcome and useful calling to mind of all of that.

Stewardship Program

Our Stewardship program is a perpetual commitment to the lands we protect. Our mission is to encourage good stewardship and management practices on the land.

Founded by foresters, Mount Grace employs practices and techniques on our land that are based on science and time-tested approaches from the fields of forestry, conservation biology and agriculture that demonstrate for the public and other conservation organizations how active and responsible stewardship can provide long-term environmental and economic rewards.

Mount Grace owns over 1,700 acres of land that are open to the public for recreational uses. As a landowner, Mount Grace has a policy of paying property taxes on all the land we own even though non-profits are exempt from these taxes.

Mount Grace management components include:
- Trail construction and maintenance
- Invasive plant control
- Wildlife and habitat monitoring
- Ecological planning
- Ecological restoration
- Sustainable habitat management

Each property is inventoried for plant communities, wildlife (especially rare and threatened species), and critical habitat for rare and declining species. Our management approach is currently focused on the properties best suited for active forest management. Our team works with a licensed consulting forester to develop long-term forest stewardship plans that integrate biodiversity conservation and climate change while practicing the sustainable harvest of forest products from our working forests.

Pair of Bald Eagles by Jeff Blanchard

Blue Heron by Jeff Blanchard

Eagle Reserve Conservation Area in Royalston

In 2016, the Solinas and Zimmerman families worked with Mount Grace and the Town of Royalston to create the Eagle Reserve Conservation Area. The name comes from a breeding pair of bald eagles that have nested near the waterside in past years.

With the help of loyal volunteers, Mount Grace has created and now maintains a total of three trails at Eagle Reserve. Listed under the Massachusetts Endangered Species Act, Blue-spotted Salamander, Wood Turtle, and the Northern Harrier have been observed on or near Eagle Reserve as part of our wildlife monitoring. Additionally, we worked with Dave Small of the Athol Bird and Nature Club to identify other bird species, such as the pied-billed grebe.

What better time, if you could put it that way, to take an adventure into wood, wildlife, water and clean bright air. The pandemic of 2020-21 sent many of us out seeking better vistas, meditation and poetry. How thankful I am to have been given the opportunity to participate in the Writing the Land project, to be able to adopt the Eagle Reserve Conservation Area, and to have Mount Grace Land Trust willing to adopt me. Peace and sanctuary were found there in three poems, on three trails in three different seasons.

Eagle Reserve on Winchenden Road in Royalston, Massachusetts is surrounded by a 139 acre Spruce-Tamarack forest and a rare patchwork floating bog, a refuge for pied-billed grebes, blue heron and hooded mergansers with sightings of rare golden eagles. The David H. Small Community Trail is an accessible 0.3 mile trail to the water with a viewing platform; Peninsula trail is a scenic 0.5 miles surrounded by woods jutting into the water pointing out distant mountains, and nearby Stone Road Trail, entered through a hayfield, is a 1/4 mile hike through a secret door to a trickling dam and views of the tails of the other two trails, forming a triangle on the water. All three trails can be explored in one day and lead from woodlands to open sky and beaver influenced wetlands.

-Candace R. Curran, July 18, 2021

Breathtaking
Mindful Guided Walk
Eagle Reserve, Mount Grace Landtrust , The David Small Community Trail
with Charlotte Weltzin and Marielena Lima
by Candace R. Curran

Beneath a brilliant ceiling   on a new snow of fallen stars
we are sent one by one down the trail into   thick woods
swallowed in the opening   ten of us   with masks and boots
hats and mittens   socially distanced   entering a crisp silence

one foot in front of the other   *one two three four five*   a broken
string of pearls   a meditative walk alone   together   hypnotic
sleepwalkers   losing our minds in nature's prayer grounds among
a woven press of paws and tails   white on white to the wooden

bridge   a stand of evergreens   *six seven*   arriving at the observation
deck   at the edge of winter's tundra   the frozen expanse of a
tamarack bog   the emptiness spread out before us   *eight nine ten*
we are crows brought to something shiny   alive to that treasure of

having lost ourselves to the refuge within   we coax ghost breath   *out*
before inviting   each new breath   *in*   before restringing the necklace
one through *ten*   to arrive back at the beginning with a bell ringing
peace   a different wilderness from where we all began

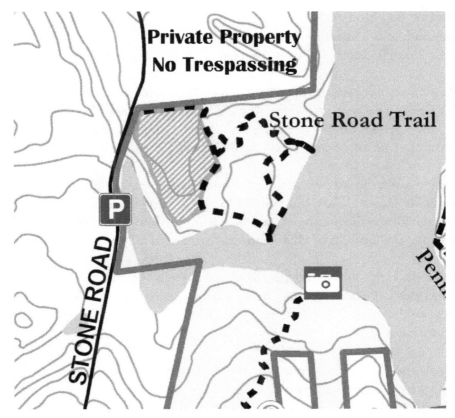

**Private Property
No Trespassing**

Stone Road Trail

STONE ROAD

Stone Road Trail
by Candace R. Curran

Head for the trail shaped like a bluebird sitting on a branch
one quarter mile down Stone Road to arrive at the hayfield
to walk along a neatly stacked stonewall   across a wide open
flowered field to trailhead   and there   look up   the blue blaze
the key to entering a sun speckled woods   filled with the who's
who of birdsong   walk the rock and needle path   unwinding
under an evergreen ceiling of boughs and the sweet smell of
clarity   the pure oxygen you had forgotten existed   to that bright
opening where sky and it's clouds have fallen into the wetlands
and a goose and gander   their goslings see you before you see them
effortlessly slip away and so do you   falling into a peace that fills
and loosens the strings of your bones   letting everything go and you
didn't know   you didn't even know   you were so tightly strung

Various Bog Monsters
by Candace R. Curran
          Eagle Reserve's Peninsula Trail

Parking across from the farmhouse   a mob of pinheaded
Far Side guinea hens   *Charge*   "Watch out for the rooster!"
a farmer grins from the door and we scramble   hustling past
comical   football-shaped fowl   herded by a bully rooster

to arrive at trailhead   presenting us with a late autumn bog
a still life walk to land's end   beaver lodges looking like empty
rentals dotting the perimeter   a trickle from the opposite shore
leaking   the location of their dam   a surround of pines

point skyward   loll on the ground pencil chewed   others
stand charred where lightning lit the narrow path   and oh this
clear cold oxygen   the sun going down beginning   hypnosis
where has it gone   the afternoon   white specks falling on

needle carpets   disappearing   we seek hibernation   a nap
shall we just sleep here until   spring-kissed   wake to a new
soundscape   the snipe's winnow   a pumper-lunk of bitterns
the bother and bite of tiny insects   their whine and whir

we walk instead   the plank   a finger peninsula   thin ice
etching water's edge   back where guinea hens   as watch-dogs
sound   ratchet up their two syllable staccato   and a brash
red-headed rooster   hackles up   runs fence between us

Farm Conservation Program

Farm conservation is a key part of Mount Grace's overall strategy for land protection. Protecting a farm not only saves open space, but also keeps local jobs and income in the rural economy. Since 1986, Mount Grace has worked to protect more than two dozen farms around the North Quabbin region, including Sunset View Farm in Winchendon. In addition to conserving farmland, Mount Grace is on the forefront of exploring new tools to help make farming viable. Under the "whole farm forever" approach, the land and its buildings are sold to farmers at an agricultural value with the goal of keeping the land in the hands of farmers forever.

Sunset View Farm in Winchendon

Owned by Chuck and Livvy Tarleton, Sunset View Farm is a 70-acre organic farm that sells fresh-picked, seasonal local produce including tomatoes, strawberries, broccoli, and even maple syrup made in the farm's sugar shack! In addition to five acres of agricultural fields, the land is rich with forests, wetlands and a hiking trail that is only accessible from the North Central Pathway.

Bordered by Route 140 on one side and by the North Central Pathway on the other, Chuck and Livvy knew that if nothing was done to protect this land, it would quickly become house lots. In 2017, Mount Grace began working with the Tarletons to protect the farm and ensure it will always be operated as a farm. Mount Grace co-holds a conservation restriction on the land with North County Land Trust. An Option to Purchase at Agricultural Value also held by Mount Grace means the next generation of farmers can purchase the land together with the house and other infrastructure at an affordable price – keeping Sunset View Farm a whole farm forever.

Passing the Torch at Sunset Farm
by Sharon A. Harmon

Pray for a good harvest,
But continue to hoe.
                    --- Irish Saying

Chuck and Livvy heeded their call forty-two years ago,
call of soil, whisper of green poking from the earth.
They listened to earth worms beneath the land.
Advised deer to keep away from their produce.

Witnessed the ever thriving, slugs, mud and droughts,
basked in the glory of fields knotted with flowers.
Black raspberries, kale, pumpkins, fun flowers,
fragrant herbs flowed each season like waves rippling.

Onions, garlic, tomatoes exploded from fields, mixed
with sweat and aching muscles. Listened to crickets
at the end of the season heralding harvest. A sunset
painted sanctuary passed to the next set of farmer's dreams.

Dreams of Farmers
by Sharon A. Harmon

Staunch New Englanders strive
to nurture earth's deep roots.
Try to overcome hard put obstacles
on this two-hundred-year-old farm.

Stone walls and the spirit of rugged hands
trail through the woodland like a maze.
Centennial hemlocks, trillium,
swamp pinks and poison ivy crawl the floor

echoing the musty woods. Deep in the souls
of hardcore farmers, the truth
grows new shoots, curling from the bones
of the land, keeps the vision in their hearts.

Farmers carry on to till, harrow, and tame
small plots that the forest begs to reclaim.
Much like the elusive endangered
Lady Slipper that delicately spreads,

the farm lands remain threatened.

Flower Haiku
by Sharon A. Harmon

Lady Slipper blooms
    Hoping for another chance
Empress of the forest

Photo: Chuck and Livvy in Farm Stand by Norm Eggert (left)

Southeast Land Trust

Exeter, NH

The Southeast Land Trust (SELT) conserves and stewards land for the benefit of people and nature in New Hampshire. SELT serves 52 towns and cities of Rockingham and Strafford counties and has conserved tens of thousands of acres since 1980, including nature preserves, hiking trails, farmland, and scenic vistas. SELT relies on its annual contributing members, committed board of directors, and talented staff and volunteers to keep advancing critical conservation initiatives in our region.

-Burley Farms-Chelsea Steinauer-Scudder
-Howard Swain Memorial Forest-Kathryn Millar
-Pawtuckaway River Reservation-Megan Buchanan
-Stonehouse Forest
    -Sarah Anderson
    -Grace Mattern
-Stout Oak Farm-Mimi White

Burley Farms

Growing
by Chelsea Steinauer-Scudder

When I first came
to these New England forests
I missed the grand sky,
the open land of the plains.

I was always trying to peek behind
the tall trees, the granite cliffs,
for a view of wide lands
that disappeared into the curve of the sky.

But we are made up of places
and the land weaves itself into us.
We wrap the seasons round, growth rings
expanding outward to meet what is there to greet us.

I stand on the edge of this field
preparing to walk into the dappled shade
of this woodland
and at last open my arms to return the embrace.

Burley Farms by Jerry Monkman - EcoPhotography

Language in Winter
by Chelsea Steinauer-Scudder

There are times when I struggle
with teaching my daughter language,
though of course this is what I am doing.
Her sounds are forming fast:
each new consonant, each vowel
as resplendent as the the northern cardinal
resting on his branch, a deep-orange sun
sinking behind the horizon of a winter ocean.
And I often rejoice.

But then there is today—
the late morning tracing gold
along the trunks of birch trees,
the soft rasping
of the beech who cling
to their leaves and sing
through dark nights, and this sense
that if I could listen with my body,
I might know more snow is coming—

I look at the plain,
unspoken wonder
on my daughter's face
and I know my language
to have come between myself
and the self that is not mine:
the self that would, if I could allow it,
disperse into the quiet forest
like the icy breath of the cardinal.

Beaver Pond
by Chelsea Steinauer-Scudder

It is the end of spring,
the evenings still curving
into impossibly longer light,
and I have left the built world
for one long moment to be here.

Here in the rain I am thinking of the creatures
who brought this water to stillness
who felled the trees
and dammed the stream
to make a home in the forest.

I am thinking:
When we dam, when we fell—
we fell ourselves, we fall from grace,
we forget that this water falling from the sky
courses through our own veins.

But here where the beavers have been at work,
the light rain falls
barely audible in the trees,
and their pond folds this gentle song into its breast
with the bright silence of a return home
after a long journey.

Howard Swain Memorial Forest

Feet on Ice
by Kathryn Millar

Surely death would ensue should the ice crack and I fall through

Surely in early March, New Hampshire, the ice won't crack
and I won't fall through

My first step sends what ifs running through my brain,
alone in the preserve
it is me
the frozen pond
and no other humans in sight

I can't remember the last time I walked on a frozen pond

I hesitate, contemplate
and boldly step out onto the ice
I put weight on one foot, test, and then move the other
Two feet on the ice and a defiant smile comes to my face
I lift my head trusting my feet and look around

Dead tree trunks rising straight up from the pond's frozen surface
Towering evergreens surrounding the perimeter connecting the pond to
the deep blue sky
The sunshine is holding its own
draws me in and warms my imagination
but it cannot warm the bitter wind that bites at all my exposed skin

More footsteps and I see animal tracks crisscross in front of me

More footsteps and I have questions about the beaver dam mid pond

More footsteps and a screeching hawk flies from behind the trees riding
high upon the thermals

More footsteps and the ice has developed a layer of slush
My breath catches in my throat
I stand as still as the pines and study my feet on ice
I regain my trust in Mother Nature's logic
to hold me as I walk on water
an ice world
on borrowed time

Another footstep and I am humbled and emboldened to be defying logic
In awe of the frozen
Something has shifted
Gifts only winter can bring

Howard Swain Memorial Forest (SELT Staff Photo)

Winter Wind
by Kathryn Millar

Winter may hide the details of spring
and steal the bounty of summer
But it also reveals horizons beyond the leafless limbs
and sets the stage for wind

Unseen but moving
The canopy swirls in choreographed circles
Burnt brown leaves bound to their branches quake
Tree trunks creak

Winter brings stillness and opens the silence
Wind brings an orchestra of sound

Hawk Over Head
by Kathryn Millar

Out from the tree line it comes
riding the thermals
a dance on the wind

I wish I could tell you what bird it is
its wing span
its mating habits
and more
but instead of speaking to my head, it speaks to my heart

I pay tribute to the bird
with my arms out wide
accepting the gift
until it is out of sight

I can't say a bird of prey feels joy
but this simple instinct of wind dancing must be the equivalent
I let my heart soar with it
I close my eyes to bear its joy with mine

Pawtuckaway

Pawtuckaway
by Megan Buchanan

It's Sunday and all the hawks are out.
White pines offer cone clusters skyward.
Here you'll find one hundred blues and greens
with surround-sound chickadees.

Mica splashes mix with ice: a brightness.
Fish hooks flash in golden grasses, clear filaments
caught in winter stalks.

The stream bubbles as it turns left, submerged
branches bob up and down in currents.
Leathery-orange oak leaves glow
under ice at the edge, white waxing moon slice
above us. A lone leaf releases, takes its time
    flips and floats
        zigzags in the wind
                pale copper lanceolate against crisp January blue -
                    takes a long time
                        to land on the water
                            where blueblack ripples undulate

Pines embrace in the brisk wind, singing.
O choir of trees, wind, clouds -
layers of matter, solid and dissolving.
Each cone a velvety Valentine of hope, an aria
of I love you in tree language,
dark knots of potential energy way up high
in the breeze. And these needles!
    soft, shimmering, pliant,
    sheltering me (thank you).

We humans make none of this magnificence!
We can only encircle, tend and care.

As the sun drops pale gold
behind birch, twin crows call across
snow's low-key sparkle in the shade.

Pawtuckaway by Pete Ingraham

Stonehouse Forest

Stonehouse Pond
by Sarah Anderson

Come ready with sturdy hiking shoes, ready to catch
and release. These wetlands and woodlands will leave you
breathless. You'll leave no trace. Let's review the rules:

Floating: encouraged
Entrance fee: no
Swimming: yes
Exploring: yes
Paddle boarding: absolutely, a must
Bathing: no
Finding inner peace: unavoidable

Come ready to cast your line, raise binoculars to your face.
Focus. Don't look away except to adjust your footing
on a rock or a root. Stand still. Stay still. Come swim,

see light and color flash against water below a granite cliff,
all 150 feet, on the pond's southwestern shore. Anglers, hikers,
cross-country skiers, trappers—you're all welcome.

No motor boat touches the water's surface. Eastern
Brook trout fill the 55-foot depth instead. Blue Gill, Chain Pickerel,
too. If you're paying attention, you'll see a map. The map's legend

will tell you in symbols of Shrub-emergent wetlands, vernal pools.
The property line will be a dash, an important mark of clarity.
You'll see a symbol for a gravel road, and another for a gate,

trail, footpath, and bridge. Come ready to the ridge
and use caution. Use caution all the way around, but not so much
that you miss the Mountain Laurel patch, the perennial stream,

or the beaver dam. Over three-hundred-year-old Black Gum trees
will surround you, shelter you. Come ready. Come wild
like the water's edge, like the sky at sundown. You know the rules.

Buffleheads on Stone House Pond
by Grace Mattern

Dark bands dart across water
raked rough by wind, low sun a line

in the limbs of white pine,
brush touch of gold

needles and seed heads on the shore.
The bellies of the buffleheads

flash silver in braided blue, their second
appearance this year — every year —

clumps of flutter and glide as ice opened
to sky, now again as steel descends

at dusk, blushed by indigo,
my rustic luck to catch them.

After the Storm
by Grace Mattern

The roadside pool is black
water trapped, taut
surface of reflected hemlock
and bleached beech yet to let go.

No one drops all of death. We
walked to that door
and turned back, the sky lit
blue in our bodies.

Now floating leaves shift
in wind-bits brushed low
branch litter cracks as we step
around a mound of dark

feathers, tufts of white
down underneath.

The Pond Speaks
by Grace Mattern

The pond says ledge
the ledge says
ridge arced east
and north
peak
an echo
in water swept
bare of wind to lap
our seat on the far shore.

Stonehouse Forest by Jerry Monkman - EcoPhotography

Stout Oak Farm

Stout Oak Farm
by Mimi White

Call me by my name
Poblano arugula leek
The sky leaning in
A pile of stones cleared by hand
Wind racing through the fencing

Before oak trees
The hill, before people
The land and rain when
The land was dry and snow
When the animals slept

Where the land dips
A sturdy farmhouse
That seems to want company
As shadows retreat up hill
As a pie cooling cools

Five boulders
Left behind like cairns
Pointing, *this way,* home—
Chokecherry aviary
Leafed out in light

Real soil, serious
Deer fencing – wildflower meadows
Leeks back in rotation
Heirloom Peppers, Carmen
Variety sweet & hot

AGRARIAN TRUST

Agrarian Trust

Nationwide

Agrarian Trust's mission is to support land access for next generation farmers. We need to chart the way forward. We need to hold our precious farmland in a trust for its best uses: sustainable food production and collective, ecological stewardship. We must also help the incoming organic leadership build on the legacy of our organic elders, many of whom have been farming for more than 30 years, and keep organic land in production. We need to support the stakeholders engaged in complex land succession, with all the accounting, estate planning, retirement planning and legal and technical assistance that is necessary. We need a national conversation that leads to action and traction for sustainable farming at the foundation of a new, just and equitable economy. Finally, we need community-centered Agrarian Commons to create democratic ownership, tenure, and equity rooted in the land, individualized to place, and connected across the country.

-Liberation Farm-David Crews
-Vernon Family Farm-Jessica Purdy
-Normanton Farm-Mary Brancaccio
-Brookford Farm-Megan Collins
-Bread and Butter Farm-Dan Close

Agrarian Trust believes that conservation is done by and for people and that people eat, hold culture, and deserve justice, and that all of these things are connected.

The protected versus unprotected farms all depends upon whose perspective is centered. A farm protected through a conservation easement may be protected against extraction and development, but not be protected for agriculture or for farmers. At the same time, a farm held in a community land trust, Agrarian Commons, or community-centered shared commons might be protected for the farmer and for agriculture, but not for conservation or environmental purposes.

Land trust work to conserve land is done because we as humans also destroy, degrade, commoditize, and extract from land. Too often, we align with this destructive, colonizing relationship with land because we have suppressed, devalued, or exterminated Indigenous and regional foodways and agrarian and Indigenous culture, and because we lack frameworks, constructs, and agreements tied to land justice.

Land conservation by land trusts is a positive action to address a negative system, yet it need not align with the systems that got us to this present-day situation. Our human existence on the earth likely cannot withstand another century of the systems we presently operate within. Indigenous and regional foodways, agrarian and Indigenous Culture, and communities tied to land have deep wisdom and practical knowledge that must guide a cultural transformation.

We seek a renewed adaptation of ancient systems and ancient relationships to the land.

Liberation Farm

On the morning of October 24, 2020 I had the privilege to meet Muhidin Libah, of the Somali Bantu Community Association, at the site of what would become (in the following year) the new Bantu community farm. The Agrarian Trust has helped Muhidin and the Bantu Association find this new land in the foothills of Wales, Maine—what is also Abenaki ancestral land. Muhidin graciously spent a few hours with me that morning talking and walking the land, and the following poem comes from our time together. It is dedicated to the spirit and will of the Somali Bantu Community Association as well as the good work of Agrarian Trust.

--David Crews, May, 2021

Liberation Farm
by David Crews

for Agrarian Trust and the Somali Bantu Community Association

1

When I pulled onto the land

that now is and will become the site for the new
Somali Bantu community farm

here, in Wales

Muhidin was feeding the goats

They were facing different directions like leaves
piled near him

among scatterings of carrots, celery, lettuces

There are no crops here yet—the rolling field
of 107 acres

that ends in a distant ridge colored by Maine's
autumn trees

will support over two hundred Somali farmers
and their families

How Muhidin came to live here has the distance
of a story

and sounds like the story of many in the Bantu
community

—a refugee at the age of seven

he remembers walking two months on a road
flooded with families in flight

through the desert

the only food that which they could carry

2

As we walk the land I wonder if Muhidin is aware
what bird species here are in decline

will he know how to handle black bears?

He scoffs at the berry-filled scat—back where
I am from, he tells me

the dogs would eat you if they could

and he does not laugh

The goats from inside their pen watch us walk by
the site where future greenhouses will be built

to grow vegetables Somali farmers know—

okra, a squash called *katito*, a type of kidney bean
called *digir*

and African eggplant, *kurere*

He says there are even some local businesses
who want their flint corn

then helps me spell *galey*

grown: four seeds, sown six feet apart, with
squash, beans, carrots nestled between

Haudenosaunee peoples tell stories of
Three Sisters

We are standing on ancestral lands

of Algonquin tribes, those who have come to
dialects of Abenaki—

Kennebec, Nanrantsouak, Arosaguntacook

Gunshots suddenly fire through neighboring
woods, and without any hunter orange

we turn and walk back toward the road

3

Muhidin was seven when General Howe visited
his elementary class

under a tent in the desert, promised they would
return to their homes soon

this, part of the UN taskforce movies speak of

But violence in and around his village in Middle
Jubba raged and powerful tribes took over

Somalis, he tells me, live in Kenya and Ethiopia
too

it was colonists who took land, drew borders

his country for as long as he remembers—
one of violence

Muhidin lived in a refugee camp for twenty years

4

One of the goats rises with big watchful eyes,
puts front hooves on the fence

without looking Muhidin strokes the goat's neck

Traditional Somali farming is farming by hand
and back home, he says

they do not compost—the growing season

a full nine months

after the monsoons come, when the river floods

and farm fields fill rich with nutrient

5

This land here in Wales

now proves the third property this community
has tried to purchase

lands for sale in the past suddenly no longer
for them

There are possibilities here, Muhidin tells me

the land large enough to support not just the
farmers and their families

but the hope to have excess food beyond crops
they donate locally

and a farmstand, a store here on site and perhaps
a catering business

A beige goat with dark ears picks up a carrot and
grinds it to meal

This time, he says, the local community in Wales
gave great support

and now, here, on this new land

they will get to celebrate *Idd* twice a year without
permit

how unfamiliar these terms—rent, lease, property

Back home Somali land is not owned or sold

and when a traveler arrives at a new village that
person is actually given

a plot—both to farm and raise a family

Muhidin tells me of traditional Somali dances

sometimes in trance, sometimes speaking
tongues

negotiations with spirit

it is both departure and arrival—*shraro, shrarow,*
borane

6

Muhidin tells me, he could be killed for returning
to his village

having acquired too much education

he will always be a refugee

His work serving the Bantu association now comes
upon fifteen years

the land here, he says, brings great joy to their
community

how an excitement these days travels among
the group like whispers

how the idea of land, and their connection to it, is
so intimately planted into a presence

of mind and body

I marvel at the energy the earth brings

Before leaving, I thank Muhidin for his time, for
meeting me

It was no problem—pleased to, he says

I'd be here for my goats

Farmers don't farm alone; they need a deep relationship with the community.

What we are doing provides land access which in turn provides wealth, health, peace,
and security---this requires a mindset and cultural shift.

Are you ready to be part of the change?

Vernon Family Farm

Chickens
by Jessica Purdy

I come to the farm in the morning. It's April
and trees are just budding, turning into leaves
that will green all summer and then go
out like sunsets in autumn. I can walk freely
past the store and into the short grass pasture
the farmhand tells me are too small for grazing
yet. When the chicks get big enough they
can roam, eating and laying eggs,
serving as fresh food for people like me
who are sad but glad to see how clean
and healthy they seem. Their white puff
bodies kept warm in the cold,
cool in the heat. On the pristine dirt floor,
they eat, sleep, perch, preen. Pink skin, feathers
coming in, they sound like water falling
in open air. I can smell the heated breath
of their climate-controlled shelter. The grown
chickens gossip and huddle, notice me.
All around me wildlife waits for no one.
Reliant on themselves, mourning doves
coo in the old maples, sing their instincts to the air.

We prioritize people, communities, food systems, AND natural spaces and ecosystems.

We protect land to put people ON it, not to keep people off of it.

*We save land from development in order to create a different kind of economic
opportunity - a sustainable, ecological, and socially just kind.*

*We are new and we are different, and we are exactly what is needed now to address
the issues of unfair land access.*

Cows at Vernon Family Farm
by Jessica Purdy

Cows chuff the hay so quietly
I can hear the mourning dove coo.
When I was a child I learned
To imitate their call, liked to think
I heard their call in response.

Next to the berm of compost,
piled wood, split trees. The work
of the farmer is evident. Mud
patterned with tractor tracks.
Dandelions spring up in the ruts.

I'm introduced to "Maeve" and "Maple"
They are being raised for milk.
Two Jersey heifers. The softest black eyes
and lashes like feathered fans.

"Clover" and "Doc" black and white
Wagyu holsteins. Dark brown "Dandelion"
will be for meat. Did the farmer's children
name them? They trundle by, little girls
guided in their father's hand. I imagine
myself as a child then, with little need of names,
whirling in my rubber boots, watching
my skirt rise in a circle around me—
my soles printed in the mud after rain.

Land Access is a Growing Problem in the United States

Land Prices have skyrocketed, but farm income has not increased as land prices have, making it impossible to pay off land debt. 40% of farmland is rented: 37 midsized farms close every day.

The average age of farmers is 62 and with 400 million acres of land expected to change hands in the next two decades, who will get to have access to that land?

Counting Sheep
by Jessica Purdy

Seven lambs, four sheep, and one llama.
The llama rubs her face on the hay.
The electric fence ticks. A reminder:
Don't Touch. The lambs sleep, seem
to smile into the sun. One rests its white
hoof on the back of a black
one. The sheep *burp* and *maa*.

One of the lambs is sick.

Somewhere a little girl pockets
little plastic farm animals
from a church playroom. When
her mother finds her with them,
she makes her give them back.
She hadn't known it was wrong
to take what didn't belong to her,
only wanted to keep
the feel of the plastic pig's smooth
side, the sheep's rough white fur,
the horse's brown flank, and play
with them a little longer.

*At this moment in our history we are faced with an unreasonably high cost of land
and an unreasonably low price of food and agricultural labor.*

How can a healthy food system be sustained under these circumstances?

*We must shift normative standards that currently define American land use, which
reward development over conservation and extraction over stewardship.*

*We are so proud to be working with farms across the country who value the land they
work and the community they feed, and who care for the soil and the people who in
turn sustain them.*

Normanton Farms

Heaven's Breath
by Mary Brancaccio

Here, human time surrenders to another keeper
of records: a greater clock measures
by tree rings and mutations, by fossil record
and ancient artifacts of Pennacook people
who farmed this land for thousands of years
before the French and English came.

Above the Merrimack, mist ghosts the waters
banks rising to rich pastures, leaves
silver-beaded as rain blesses a thirsty earth.
Morning showers invite a bird feast:
robins, longspurs, crows and bluebirds
flit through the meadow, hunting worms
and beetles among its grasses. Its sheaves
are thick and glossy, seed heads fat
and firm. Among blades of winter rye,
buttercups, red clover and bluets.
Further on, a wild sprinkling of
yellow birdsfoot and purple lupine.

Below the hill, a herd of cattle
bellows melodies of birth and nurture.
Four cows with new calves keep
their distance as I approach the fence.
One heifer gambols across the pasture
kicking her heels in a show of agility
before curiosity gets the better of her
and she circles back to greet me,
nostrils flaring to catch my scent.

Two redwings light on fence posts.
Trilling, they take to the air in wide arcs
skimming trees beneath purple-grey clouds.
Hens nestle wing to wing on grass in open-air

coops. Cheeping softly, they seem contented
by their flock's warmth on a cool morning
as if the business of the day were rest
and conversation, as they wait out the rain.

Along the pasture's edge, a creek
courses over granite, strumming
notes of its own design. Fiddleheads
open as lush fronds. Along the mossy banks
families of pines: mother trees sheltering
nurslings, their branches greening with growth.

I wait and listen as ancient rhymes flicker
from root to root. This is a healing land.
Its wisdom runs deep.

Imagine a Fence
by Mary Brancaccio

"[T]he land no longer nursed the river in its bosom, but they con-
versed as equals…"

Henry David Thoreau, *A Week on the Concord and
Merrimack Rivers*

A wild call lures me to this fertile land
hands me a shovel and urges me to dig, no
not to dig, to learn to use a meadow longer
than one season, the way the earth has nursed
all life with patience. Imagine a fence as a river
or better, a canoe, drifting through hills, down valleys in
measured steps, so that the cattle graze its
bounty, and in return enrich this loamy bosom
that suckles so many living things, but
with wise moderation. Concealed in cow piles, they
seed new grass, as if the spring and fall conversed
then weighed the balance of reap and sow, as
on a purser's scale and found them equals.

Self-Portrait as a Crosby Fledgling
by Mary Brancaccio

An old woman lifts me from among hundreds
and I am alarmed, flapping and cackling

though she holds me fast, tucking
my featherless wings against her chest until I quiet.

Once, I used my egg-tooth to break free
of what confined me. To birth oneself

is arduous work. It started with an urge
to crack my shell, to sip the air outside.

Soon I learned I was not alone. Hundreds
if not thousands of other chicks

had done this work as well. A generation
of featherless offspring, we looked

strange to one another, our wings bony
and bare. The world was cold and threatening

until we learned to band together, a flock
of flightless creatures, pitifully gangly.

But time grew us quills and downy feathers
that gave our wings some use: small flights

that led to perches, a place of comfort
and safety. Between my beak and claws

I can defend myself most days against
the hawk and skunk, mad killers

of my kind. The meaning of life eludes me:
so many of my days are spent chasing

food and shelter, water and food.
And warmth and company. It's not

what I would call a rarified existence.
I live in an eat-or-be-eaten world.

The ones who eat have two eyes
front and center. The prey see

side to side, so as to spot what's coming.
I turn one eye toward the woman.

Her two eyes gaze at me. She looks
like an eater, but she is cooing

as if somewhere inside her lives
a feathered soul. Our eyes lock

I can feel the pulse in her fingertips
against my body -- my heartbeat

is faster than hers, my lungs fill
and empty to a quicker pace

but for this moment, we see
eye-to-eye. Then she lets me go

and I fly into the circle of my flock.
It's hella confusing getting singled out.

Owning land gives you power, leverage, and control. We're not interested in having that for ourselves. What we are doing is securing land and then GIVING it BACK to COMMUNITIES. Communities need to be empowered, they need forms of leverage to bring wealth and prosperity to themselves and their neighbors, and they deserve control over their own spaces and futures. The Agrarian Commons is a necessary and innovative approach to address the realities of how land is owned, tenure and equity are conveyed, and land stewardship is carried out.

Brookford Farm

Tranquility
by Megan Collins

far as eye can see
By the river underneath the trees
Tiny shop has honey from bees
Sky so blue
Earth so green
Dogs at play as plants breathe

Cows and cream
Veggies and cheese
Love nature
Live with her
And you shall
Receive
Tranquility

Free
by Megan Collins

Water runs constantly
Never taking a breath
Roots run deep
Never stopping to rest
Come down to Brookford farm Please be our guest
The trees and plants breath Feel truly blessed
Never seen so much green Never felt so serene
This is how it must be To feel like you are free

Bread and Butter Farm

The Life of a Farmer
by Dan Close

You wake up in the morning
Just before you go to bed
And you hit the sack in evening-time
But before you rest your head
You hear the rooster crowing
In the pre-dawn morning light
And you realize time means nothing,
It's the farmer's daily plight.

> But while the land is fertile
> While the earth is good
> You must keep on working
> In the fields and in the wood.
> > Yes, while the land is fertile
> > While the earth is good
> > It demands that you stand up
> > And work it as you should.

So it's up and rise 'fore sun-up
It's what the cows demand
It's all a part of working
On each farm across the land
And while each lonely farmer
Starts his daily milking chores,
The cows are always willing
To produce a little more.

> But while the land is fertile
> While the earth is good
> We must keep on working
> In the fields and in the wood
> > Yes while the land is fertile
> > While the earth is good
> > It demands that we get up
> > And work it as we should.

Maple in the springtime,
Haying in the summer sun,
Cutting sheets of ice in blocks
For the summertime's long run
Tending to the animals,
Mending fence and rail,
Got to keep on gittin'
Or the critters will prevail.

    But while the land is fertile
    While the earth is good
    We must keep on working
    In the fields and in the wood
        Yes while the land is fertile
        While the soil is good
        It demands that we go out
        And work it as we should.

While our backs are breaking
With the burdens of the day
Still we have to look up
And figure why we stay
The scent of good turned farm soil
The patter of the rain
The colors of the rainbows
Are why some of us remain

    And while the land is fertile
    While the earth is good
    We must keep on working
    In the fields and in the wood
        Yes while the land is fertile
        While the soil is good
        We will keep on working
        In the fields and in the woods.

Through hail and snow and fire
And a billion locusts more

Though across our land they travel
And plague us evermore,
We cannot leave the land we love,
We cannot leave our farms
Until ten thousand bales of hay
Are safe within our barns.

      And while the land is fertile,
      While the earth is good,
      We must keep on working
      In the fields and in the wood.
          Yes, while our soil is fertile,
          While our land is good,
          We will keep on working
          In the fields and in the woods.

Garth the Big
by Dan Close

(upon viewing the Bread and Butter Farm's video of the pig herd heading off to its summer pasture)

Oh, Garth the Big was a mighty fine pig
With a mighty fine curlicue
On his mighty fine tail. When he'd give it a whirl
He could stir up quite a stew

With a hint of mischief in his bright blue eyes
He'd wink, give a grin or two
And an 'Oink!' would emerge from deep below,
Somewhere near his heart, just for you.

For Garth the Big was a big-hearted pig;
Had a heart that was true-blue
And one fine day in the merry month of May

Garth met a young sow named Sue
Who was destined to become the grandmother of one
Great big pen of piglets. It's true!

Well Sue took the heart of that big wild boar
And turned him into a puddle
Of blubbering pathos enlaced with bathos
And blithering porcine stew.

"Oh, won't you come gambol and snarfle with me",
Said Garth the Big to Sue
"I can see you like edibles sloppy and wild,
Like mushrooms and acorns and beechnuts too.

"I know a spot where pig dreams are born.
It's up on that hill in the forest.
We'll feast on chanterelles, that rhymes with bells
That will play on our wedding day,

"And there we'll stay, wile the summer away,
Midst the walnuts and hazelnuts, too,
And fungo porcino and champignons
With shitakes, enokis, and portobellos
And morels, and hen-of-the-woods, woo-hoo!

And if we are lucky, my sow young and plucky,
We may snuffle around and root out of the ground
Some funky and muskkevous black truffles, too.
A paradise we'll find, my one Sue sublime
This is my promise to you."

And to this day, they oink away
In perfect pig bliss and true,
And coming in spring, while bluebirds sing,
A litter of piglets for two.

The Breed from Devonshire
by Dan Close

We are the Red Breed of Devon,
The oldest breed on Earth
To have been stamped and measured
From horn to tail to girth.

'Twas in the Shire of Devon –
That's the place that we called home,
Where mighty ancient herds were born.
We're Red Devon to the bone.

But we left the land of Camelot,
We went a'sea and roamed,
And when we found Australia's sunny shores
We were set to call it home.

But suddenly up and at it again,
Once more we sailed the seas,
And to America's shores we came
And now we do graze free.

In these pastures of the Green Hills
We graze the lush green grass
And helping to make this land we're on
We chew our cud *en masse*.

And in the course of nature's way
We finish what we've chewed;
We leave our little gifts behind.
(Oh, please don't think us rude!)

We're only doing naturally
What nature has intended
To make the grasses green once more,
And make us, too, contented.

We are not large, by any means,
Like Holsteins or like Jerseys tended
Who have been turned to milk machines,
Their udders great distended.

We do not live in grand new barns
With thousand other bovines bound,
For we live free, as it should be,
And revel in kind nature's charms.
No, we are not great clompers,
But with our smaller tread
We gently graze upon the earth
And make the earth our bed.

Oh, we are blessed, we must confess,
To sojourn happily here;
To go about our duties
And hold our land so dear.

And some of us are hornless,
While some of us are horned,
And some of us get horny,
Which is how our calves get borned,

But lest you think us racy
And lest you think us wild
We're simply quite good-natured
With dispositions mild.

And in conclusion, let us say
Before another thought we utter,
"Upon this land we'll make our stand,
For it is our Bread and Butter."

Valley Community Land Trust

Franklin County, MA

Valley Community Land Trust
-Poet: Paul Richmond

The Valley Community Land Trust (VCLT) is based in Franklin County Massachusetts. VCLT owns land that it leases to home-owner lessees, whose rights to use the land and own their homes are governed by 99 year leases.

VCLT acquired most of its current land at a time when it was a pioneer in the area's land conservation efforts. Most of the land was originally funded by several large donations.

VCLT's lessees are mostly those who have self-financed and often self-built their homes, or, over time, have bought those homes from previous lessees. Usually, this occurs without financial assistance from the VCLT beyond the provision of the land. The organization is currently financed entirely through its lease fees and occasional small donations; and conducts its administration primarily with volunteer labor from the lessees themselves.

VCLT lessees and other members are united by a belief that since
land is not the creation of human effort, it is fundamentally unjust for
individuals to profit from the buying and selling of land. By holding
a stock of land in trusteeship, never again to be bought and sold, we
seek to add a measure of equability to the imbalances that challenge our
world.

Valley Community Land Trust
by Paul Richmond

Has a long history
Of having a political consciousness
Anti War
Self Reliance
Back to the land
Economic justice
Women's rights
Anti Racist
Core value
No One Owns Land

You are leasing a piece of the earth
While you are here
A place to live
Being a steward
On the land
In the beginning
There were hippie handshakes
Statements of values
By-laws and meetings
VCLT was incorporated in 1977
Over 200 acres of land in Franklin County, MA.
Taken off the market
The land provides homes for more than 50 people
Homes with
Gardens
Woods
Orchards
Open fields
And cottage industries
Sustaining an organization for the last 44 years
Isn't all parties and potlucks
More of a roller coaster
Of ups and downs
Individuals and group energy
In a dance with our daily lives
And our commitment
To the VCLT
By signing a lease
A number of the original members have died
Others have moved on
New younger members
Taking care of the land
That the earth is not for sale
We come into this world
And along with all the other creatures who are here
Finding our way to be sustainable
Taking care of the land for future generations
The land is not for sale

On The Land
by Paul Richmond

There are memories
Of dreams
Of families
Of planting an orchard
Having one's own artist's studio
Where the dog is buried
Where the barn was raised
Where aunt Judy fell and broke her leg
The outdoor dinner parties
When we all danced in the field
Under the moon light
Planting
Feeding the earth
Making a home for bees
For future stewards to enjoy
Constantly reminding ourselves
That our work and living on the land
Doesn't mean we own it
Instead deepening our connection
To the earth where we go to rest
Be reborn as the flowers
For the next stewards

How Much For The Land
by Paul Richmond

I'll give you some beads
I'll give you some shells

At $25 not many could afford it

At $100 you were grateful
You didn't have to pay $200

At an auction I bid $2000
And felt victorious

At $50,000
I was told it was a steal

At $100,000
I was told to appreciate the quality

At $500,000
I was told I had good taste

At a Million
I was told I had privilege

At a Billion
I was told I had power

At a trillion dollars I watched it burn
At a trillion dollars I watched it burn
When the smoke cleared
It wasn't worth anything
To anyone

I knew it from the beginning
There is no dollar amount
The earth is not for sale
Why did I play along

Annual Meetings
by Paul Richmond

The gathering of the members
Over the years
Potluck dinners
Rotating to the various leaseholds
With work days
To help each other with our projects
There is the sense of family
Of being involved with others
In a common cause
Then there is the craziness of each of our lives
Losing of jobs
Being behind in lease fees
Internal battles for power
Over what is the organization
Which is all of us
As years go by
Disagreements
Changes in ideology
Not as easy as just walking away
All the land is connected
Needs to be protect and maintained by VCLT
We are VCLT

Having to find ways to work things out
Attempts to come to a consensus
And when it is not possible
How to move on
For the survival of the organization
Accepting things change
What worked 20 years ago
May not work now
Takes attention and work
To keep an organization up to date
As land prices keep rising
Due to overpopulation
Due to climate changes
Will there be a scarcity of inhabitable places to live
Where there is water
Not extreme heat or cold
There is a lot that has to change
In our culture as to how we view
The earth
And will countries stop
Marking off areas
That they say are theirs
Scarcity has always played a part
We have managed to keep
VCLT alive and well
Keeping land off the open market
See you at the next semi-annual meeting

Monadnock Community Land Trust

Wilton, NH

Monadnock Community Land Trust Mission

The mission of the Monadnock Community Land Trust is to hold land in trust for the larger community. We promote ecologically responsible use of that land and offer possibilities for affordable housing for low to moderate income families. Our intention is to protect the environment, promote the health and vitality of local communities, and promote diversity by offering access to land.

Hearthstone Community Association Mission

At Hearthstone we strive to promote ecologically responsible use of the land. We hold the land in a manner that conserves resources and protects the environment for the good of the earth and the community. We have developed methods of home ownership consistent with the above intentions and strive to foster a community of people living and working together for the well-being of the earth, the community, and the individuals living there.

-Poet: Patrice Pinette

Monadnock Community Land Trust & Hearthstone Community

Monadnock Community Land Trust was founded in 1977 with the purpose of removing land from the speculative market and preserving local geography. At the same time, the Hearthstone Community Association was being formed by local families looking for affordable housing. Eventually, the two groups began working together. Since that time, the Hearthstone Community has been located on land which is owned and stewarded by Monadnock Community Land Trust.

The Vision

Founded in 1978, Hearthstone is an intentional community of adults and children from diverse backgrounds who are dedicated to creating a safe, nurturing environment where residents seek to live in harmony with the natural world and each other. Common values include: embracing diversity, governing together by consensus, walking softly on the earth and committing to living these values within the context of daily community life.

The Story

Back-to-the-land, build your own house, live together in community, save the earth, love everybody right now. These all swirled in the air in the late 1960's and early 70's. Such hopes even blew through a small, rural hamlet in Southern New Hampshire during a watercolor painting workshop at a local high school. Lunch time conversations among the participants revealed that three families were all looking for the same thing—affordable land on which to build a house.

One individual knew of a farm going on the market but with the stipulation that it not be subdivided. The property had a large house and barn on approximately 200 acres so was beyond any price range the three families could imagine. Although subdividing was unacceptable to the owner, negotiations continued. Eventually, the owner realized that he had already subdivided one portion of the property, separating it from the land with the house and barn. This piece of the property gave the group the road frontage that they needed without a large financial burden. This then became the solution to the quest for land.

As word spread, more families joined. An initial meeting was held on August 17, 1978. After information about the property and personal ideals were shared, it was time to get realistic. What about financial realities? With amazing transparency, as some people were meeting others for the first time, all present openly shared their financial situations—what resources they could contribute to the project, what they could loan to the project, what resources they might have going into the future either for the community or to sustain themselves personally. One individual offered a substantial loan which made it possible to consider going forward. A core group continued to meet weekly to explore ways to purchase the land as families dropped out and new families joined. This group met weekly for the next 5 years.

Mailboxes in July by Sherry Jennings

During this same time period two members of the group became involved with another initiative which was forming a land trust to remove parcels of land from the speculative market and thus preserve and protect some of the local geography. Eventually, the Monadnock Community Land Trust (MCLT) was born although it did not yet have any land under its auspices. To the members of both organizations it soon became obvious that the two groups could only benefit by combining. The land trust had no land while the housing group had found land but did not want to own it. With financial help from members of the housing group, MCLT purchased the land already being considered and then leased it to the housing group which became known as the Hearthstone Community Association (HCA). The members chose the name HEARTHSTONE because it contains many words that were meaningful to those pioneers—heart, hearth, art, ear, hear, earth, stone, tone, one.

When all paperwork was complete, the Monadnock Community Land Trust, a nonprofit organization, held the title to the 92-acre parcel which it leased to the Hearthstone Community Association. In turn each individual family enters into a renewable, inheritable, long-term lease agreement with Hearthstone. A member's leasehold includes the land under the house and the area around it called a responsibility area, which the homeowner cares for. The community as a whole in conjunction with MCLT is responsible for the land not directly surrounding the individual homes.

Once the purchase was completed, families began the work to clear the land and build their houses. Even before the first tree was cut from the heavily wooded property, all members and their children camped out there to honor the land and the elemental forces at work there.

Hearthstone Community is now over 40 years old. Twelve houses have been built on 10 of the 92 acres; the remainder is forested and used for recreation and a wood lot. Initially each house was designed and built by a family, involving contractors to a greater or lesser degree. In addition to the ideals concerning stewardship of land and providing affordable opportunities for access to land, the original members held as important the values of openness concerning financial matters, working by consensus, a willingness to share honestly during tense dialogues or conflicts as a vehicle to support personal growth and the well-being of the community, and a willingness to learn to work together in a group.

Through the years, houses have passed from one family to another until at the present only one of the original members lives at Hearthstone. Ask her and she will tell you what living at Hearthstone has meant to her.

Photo: Winter Pond by Nancy Wallace (left)

Hearthstone is a place...

• where you can step outside your door and be in nature relaxing—restoring body, mind, and spirit

• where you can look through your windows and see smoke rising from the chimneys of your neighbors and know that all is well

• where children can grow in a place that is safe with streams and woodland paths to explore

• where community is not always easy but is important.

• where neighbors gladly come to your aid whether jump starting your car, delivering meals when there is illness, or being at your side as you mourn or celebrate

• where you can find peace and solace

• where you can learn about and converse with plants, animals, rocks and trees

• where you can garden, head off into the woods, or follow your nose around a labyrinth

• where work days to care for the earth are as important as picnics at the pond

• where people are born, people die and there is the possibility for living a healthy life

• where you can care for the land even as you respect that you cannot own it

Hearthstone, like any organism, has gone through periods of growth and development and periods of rest and sleep. As with any of group of individuals living together, what goes on depends upon the members who are residing there, what are their interests, what skills do they bring. With initial projects completed and new members arriving, in recent years there has been a renewed interest and activity in beautification of the land with new gardens and landscaping areas being developed. One specific focus has been to provide plantings which invite wildlife and beneficial insects to share the land with the people. Hearthstone is also a certified New Hampshire Tree Farm.

Community social life flourishes at Hearthstone with pot-luck picnics at the pond, festival celebrations, knitting nights, bonfires, groups walking the trails together, cross country skiing, snowshoeing, and practical spring and fall clean-up-the-land days. If a family is in crisis, members come forward with care and support. If there is a flat tire or no flour for the birthday cake, a neighbor will gladly lend a hand. Hearthstone is a welcoming place to raise children—land to roam, streams to dam, forts to build and for the parents there are other adult eyes and hands to support them. As with any group of human beings working together, conflicts and disagreements arise. Over the years, individuals have become more skillful in navigating these rocky waters as community members strive to live together in peace and harmony. As life goes along, both laughter and tears abound at Hearthstone.

----Sherry Jennings

☼

Birches over the Pond by Sherry Jennings

Birch
by Patrice Pinette

May I call you sister, my neighbor, whose calm
at the core should be mine. I want your stillness,
the slightest rustle of feather-veined leaves
in the breeze, to be unafraid of danger, thunder
and lightning in the woods. Or do you shiver,
as I do? Growing older, I dream of slipping
out of my green dress for gold, then to be brave,
fine boned and patient in the cold. Bed of winter.
Rooted at last in something vaster than myself.
What essence passes from one life to another?
What language might we share of roots and reach,
shade and shimmer. Silver. By midsummer,
when wild roses bloom, your bark, marked
by subtle script, curls, peels back. Pages turning.

Hearthstone
by Patrice Pinette

We come for simplicity,
harmony with land and sky,
a dream, a drive, a need,
a knowing from inside
a parcel of the world
we can walk by trails
at twilight—shadows
in dialogue, human and owl
calling back and forth
until the clearing.

We call this land home,
intimate, not owned.
From boulders of snow
to star-strewn paths
of mountain laurel,
our senses keep time,
catch scents of coming
storms mingled with woodsmoke,
hemlock after rain, roses,
mown grass—taking in
sweetness and breathing out
awe for all that's come
before us. Glacial shaping
gave the earth its contours,
borders. Old stone walls
tell stories. Don't forget
the oak harvest, how
the horse-logger's blind horse
led the way beyond
our woods, as we made
an inroad into wildness.

We practice balance walking
labyrinths, one drawn on earth

and another etched into the heart.
Trouble is, even quiet minds
bring old fears, and nearsighted
cares can snare one another;
secrets kept come into play.
Nothing escapes place, acres
deep, but becomes it, and
evolves. Listening to dialects
of the elements, we heal
by calendula, bee balm,
and birdsong at dawn.
Neighboring creatures
cross the land to their own
purposes—deer, opossums,
hawks and crows, bears,
skunks, turkeys and coyotes.
From cold snaps to heat
waves, the winds pass
through, refreshing, bending,
breaking, and scattering dust, leaves,
film of pollen on the fire pond
rippling out and back from
man-made banks.

Enamored every day
by turn of seasons, we wait
to see what's possible.
We come to be alive, not
innocent. Change, unchanging,
soothes and outwaits us,
yielding what it must,
remaining, but for love,
untouched. In the meadow,
milkweed seeds burst
and drift into fertile beds
to rest and take root.

Exchanging breath in a web
so all-inclusive, even this
handful of houses, blessed
and bowed by births and deaths
is held and holding steady,
letting go of one world
for another, by the flower.
Still, for all that, and because
our shadows lengthen, rays also fall,
not only on stone walls and forest floor,
but slant through us, like the nature
of a truth we come to find—
transforming what we thought
we knew—until more gentle
and fiercely clear, flawed, finite,
and deeply grateful, we belong here.

The Woods Road by Sherry Jennings

Prayer to the Land
by Patrice Pinette

You are good to us
we try
loving you
to do our best for the next
generations
and for you

we turned the brown hillside
green
glad to return a favor
small gestures
humbled as we are
by you

you must know
we speak and listen deeply
to your voices
and to your leanings
to glean how far to go
with you

seeding gardens
making glades
in the near woods
where more light can stream
through
and into you

until we turn off the last
lamp
still awake to the forest
breathing
the endless presence
of you

Hearthstone in the Words of the People Living Here Now

Lines of the following poem have been selected and edited from seasonal poems written at Hearthstone meetings. At these meetings members contributed one line about each season.

A YEAR AT HEARTHSTONE

warm sun, black flies,
opening windows, cleaning, painting
pink petal blessings,
soft breeze, smell of warm earth,
blooming, bursting, bugs.
hummingbirds return, frogs sing at night.

hot, humid, cool and sunny,
green abundance, goes too fast
flowers, flowers
lush ivy's poisonous and pretty
sunshine, flowers, veggies galore,
hollow log fires.

golden sunlight, crisp air
color, color everywhere
crimson carpet, pure blue sky
crunchy apples, acorn caps
leafy roads and rustling paths
joyful dance of leaves, silent sunlight.

winter wonderland, starry nights,
tiny diamonds, endless white
Snow, snow, where can we go?
at the neighbor's we'll be, sipping hot tea
peace as the snow drops
and drifts over the land.

Hollow Log Fire by Nancy Wallace

What is Hearthstone?

Hearthstone is the people who have supported the community either in helping to form it or keep it going, people who spent hours and dollars to enable it to come into being.

Hearthstone is an ever-evolving community of individuals striving to find balance between family autonomy and community well-being within an environment of mutual care and support.

Hearthstone is the story of the people who had the vision, of the people who wanted to live here but never did, of the people who have lived here, of the people living here now and the people who will come in the future.

Hearthstone is a place for fellowship, friendship, community building, raising children, retiring, for stewarding land. It is a place for learning about one's self and the world.

Hearthstone is a place for experiencing the circle of giving and receiving.

A Wagon Load by Nancy Wallace

Poets' Biographies

Sarah Anderson holds an MFA in poetry from the Warren Wilson Program for Writers. She teaches English at Berwick Academy, and with her husband, she owns and operates The Word Barn in Exeter, NH, a gathering space for literature and music. Her poems have appeared in various journals, including *December Magazine, Raleigh Review,* and *North American Review.* She is the author of *We Hold On To What We Can* (Loom Press, 2021).

Mike Bove is the author of two books of poetry: *Big Little City* and *House Museum.* He lives in Portland, Maine with his family.

Mary Brancaccio is a poet and a teacher published in *Edison Literary Review, Minerva Rising, Naugatuck River Review, Adanna, Chest* and other journals, and in two international anthologies. Her chapbook, *Mistress of Buttons & Keys* was a finalist in Minerva Rising's "Dare to Be" poetry chapbook contest. Her first book-length collection of poetry is *Fierce Geometry.* Her poem, "A Door Ajar," has been selected for the 2021 Moving Words collaborative project with ARTS By The People.

Megan Buchanan is a poet, performer, collaborative dancemaker, teacher and activist. Her collection *Clothesline Religion* (Green Writers Press, 2017), was nominated for the 2018 Vermont Book Award. Find her work in *The Sun Magazine, A Woman's Thing,* and elsewhere. She's grateful for support from the Vermont Arts Council, Vermont Performance Lab, and the Vermont Studio Center. www.meganbuchanan.net

Tom Butler, a conservationist and writer, is the author, editor, or coeditor of more than a dozen books including *Wildlands Philanthropy, Plundering Appalachia, Protecting the Wild,* and *On Beauty: Douglas R. Tompkins—Aesthetics and Activism.* He formerly edited *Wild Earth* journal, was vice president for conservation advocacy at Tompkins Conservation, and was a past board president of Northeast Wilderness Trust. He currently serves as the Trust's senior fellow.

Robert Carr is the author of *Amaranth*, (Indolent Books, 2016) and *The Unbuttoned Eye* (3: A Taos Press., 2019) Among other publications his poetry appears in the *American Journal of Poetry, Massachusetts Review, Rattle, Shenandoah* and *Tar River Poetry*. Robert is poetry editor with Indolent Books and recently retired from a career as Deputy Director for the Bureau of Infectious Disease and Laboratory Sciences at the Massachusetts Department of Public Health. Robertcarr.org

Dan Close is a poet and novelist living in the hills of northwestern Vermont. He is the author of a book of poetry entitled *What the Abenaki Say about Dogs*, which chronicles the lives, past and present, of the Abenaki of the Champlain Basin. It will soon be available in an audio version. His novel *The Glory of the Kings* was awarded Best In Fiction prize by Peace Corps Writers. He currently serves on the board of the Poetry Society of Vermont. Danclose.net

Meghan (Meg) Collins lives in Plymouth, New Hampshire and is a senior History major at Plymouth State. Writing has been an outlet for her for most of her life, poetry being a favorite. She sings in a band called Out of Water and they write all their own music. She would love to use her voice to help the cause of preserving the land, because its more important than ever to project positive energy into that which matters— like protecting the Earth's life and ecosystems through art.

Swift Corwin has written poetry and been a photographer for over 40 years. His work can be found in several unpublished collections called *The Problem with Poetry parts 1,2, and 3*. He takes his inspiration by his day job as a consulting forester working out of Peterborough, NH.

David Crews is a writer, editor, and wilderness advocate who currently resides in southern Vermont / ancestral lands of Mohican and Abenaki peoples. He cares for work that engages a reconnection to land and place, wilderness, preservation, nonviolence. He currently serves as managing editor for *Wild Northeast*. Davidcrewspoetry.com

Candace R. Curran is founder and organizer of collaborative word-and-image multimedia exhibitions including *INTERFACE*, and *Exploded View*. She was twice named Western Massachusetts Poet's Seat

Laureate. Publications include, *Bone Cages*, an anthology, and *Playing in Wrecks* (Haley's Press), as well as journals *Raw NerVZ, Meat For Tea*, and *Silkworm*. Candace engineers word and image on the Buckland side of the Iron Bridge in Shelburne Falls, Massachusetts.

Ann Bemis Day started writing about nature in the early grades. She married Frank Day in 1970 and moved to the Mad River Valley in Vermont where they and their two children taught skiing, riding and how to care for the land and the animals who live there. Her favorite occupation is tromping around in the woods. Their farm was the first property conserved by the Vermont Land Trust. She has published several books of poetry, farming and caring for the land.

Alice B. Fogel was the New Hampshire poet laureate from 2014-2019. Her collections include *A Doubtful House; Interval: Poems Based on Bach's "Goldberg Variations"; Nothing But*, & *Strange Terrain*, a guide to appreciating poetry. Nominated 12 times for the Pushcart, she received a fellowship from the National Endowment for the Arts, among other awards, & her poems have appeared in many journals & anthologies, including *Best American Poetry*. She hikes mountains whenever possible.

Katherine Hagopian Berry (she/her) has appeared in the *Café Review, Rise-Up Review, Feral,* and *Glass: Poets Resist*, among other places. Her first collection, *Mast Year*, was published in 2020. She is a poetry reader for *The Maine Review*.

Sharon Harmon is both a poet and a freelance writer. She has written for *The Uniquely Quabbin Magazine* and also has a children's picture book coming soon. She has two chapbooks of poetry, *Wishbone in a Lightning Jar* and *Swimming with Cats*. Sharon teaches classes on writing and poetry as well as marketing. She recently published in *Compass Roads* and *Chicken Soup for the Soul*. She is an avid hiker and camper and lives deep in the woods of Royalston.

Hope Jordan grew up in Chittenango, NY. She holds a dual BA from Syracuse and an MFA from UMass Boston. Her poems have appeared in *Nine Mile, Comstock Review*, and *Naugatuck River Review*, among other publications. A longtime member of the Concord, NH-based Yogurt Poets writing group, she was the first official poetry slam master in New

Hampshire, and co-founded what is now Slam Free or Die in 2006. Her chapbook is *The Day She Decided to Feed Crows*. hopejordan.pressfolios.com

Sylvia Karman's work has appeared in *Delmarva Review, Blueline,* and *Amethyst Review,* among others. She lives in the New York Adirondack mountains and in central Maryland where she hikes and writes for the love of the journey. Currently, Sylvia is querying her first novel and working on her second. www.sylviakarman.com

Kathy Kremins (she/her) is a Newark, NJ native of Irish immigrant parents and a retired teacher. She is the author of *The Ethics of Reading: The Broken Beauties of Toni Morrison, Arundhati Roy, and Nawal el Sadaawi,* and a book of poetry, *Undressing the World,* forthcoming (Finishing Line Press, 2022). Kathy's work appears in *The Night Heron Barks, Moving Words 2020 project, Lavender Review, Divine Feminist: An Anthology of Poetry & Art By Womxn and Non-Binary Folx,* and *Too Smart to be Sentimental.*

Lori Landau (She/her, Ki/Kin) is an interdisciplinary artist. Her work is grounded in her contemplative practices and training in compassionate integrity. Her writing can be found in a variety of magazines, anthologies and blogs, and her art has been shown on both coasts. She holds an MFA in Interdisciplinary Arts from Goddard College with a concentration in Decolonial Arts Praxis. www.Lorilandauart.com

Christopher Locke's poems, stories, and essays have appeared in numerous magazines including *The North American Review, The Literary Review,* and *The Sun.* He won the 2020 Black River Chapbook Award for *25 Trumbulls Road,* and is the recipient of the D. S. Rosenberg Poetry Award, and Poetry Fellowships from Fundacion Valparaiso (Spain) and PARMA (Mexico). He teaches at The Poetry Barn, North Country Community College, and Ray Brook Federal Prison.

Rodger Martin authored *For All The Tea in Zhōngguó* (2019), *The Battlefield Guide,* (2010, 2013) and *The Blue Moon Series,* (2007) chosen by Small Press Review as a pick of the year. He is a New Hampshire State Council on the Arts roster artist. He received an Appalachia award for poetry, a NHSCAs award for fiction, fellowships from The National Endowment for the Humanities. His work has appeared in journals and anthologies throughout the U.S. and China. www.rodgerwriter.com

Grace Mattern's poetry and prose have been published widely, including in *The Sun, Calyx, Prairie Schooner, Brevity Blog* and *Yankee*. She has received fellowships from the New Hampshire State Arts Council and Vermont Studio Center and been nominated for Best of the Net and Pushcart Prizes. Her book *The Truth About Death* won the NH Readers' Choice Award 2014. Mattern also creates visual/sculptural poetry, integrating image and text in collages and hand-bound books. Gracemattern.com

Michael Mauri is a practicing forester working in the hills which make up the Connecticut River watershed of Western Massachusetts. Mike has self-published numerous small books of poetry to give away freely in person or to sell for a dollar, including *Any Timber Up There?* He occasionally reads his poetry at farmer's markets with local band Rob Skelton's Pitchfork. https://soundcloud.com/milelong

Lis McLoughlin, PhD (director of the Writing the Land project; editor) produces the annual *Authors and Artists Festival* online, as well as various poetry readings, book launches, workshops on writing with the land, and other events through her green online event/media company NatureCulture. She lives off-grid in Northfield, Massachusetts and part-time in Montréal, Québec. https://nature-culture.net

Kathryn Millar is an educator, writer, farmer, artist, and friend. She was a middle school teacher for 15 years. She has been a nomadic van dweller for many years and has traveled 49 states in the US (save Hawaii) and is well traveled abroad. She loves a good road trip and finding awe in any adventure! Kathryn has written poetry across these journeys, and throughout her life, connecting with land, people, and spirit.

Rachelle Parker is a Nassawadox born, Brooklyn bred writer. She was selected winner of the Furious Flower Poetry Prize and won third prize in the Allen Ginsberg Poetry Award. She is a fellow of Tin House Summer Workshop Poetry. Her work appears in *About Place Journal, Rhino Poetry, Paterson Literary Review, The Adirondack Review* and the anthology *The BreakBeat Poets: Black Girl Magic*. Her photographic work debuted in the Spring 2021 issue of *Orion Magazine*.

Patrice Pinette is inspired by the alchemy that arises in collaboration with other artists, writers, and musicians. She is currently an adjunct at Antioch University and a facilitator with New Hampshire Humanities. Patrice received her MFA from Vermont College of Fine Arts, and her poems have appeared in *Poet Showcase: An Anthology of New Hampshire Poets; The Inflectionist Review; Poetica; Evening Street Review; Hampden-Sydney Poetry Review; COVID Spring / Granite State Pandemic Poems,* and elsewhere.

Dawn Potter was a 2020 finalist for the National Poetry Series. She directs the Frost Place Conference on Poetry and Teaching and is the author of 8 books of poetry and prose—most recently, *Chestnut Ridge.* Her poems and essays have appeared in the *Sewanee Review,* the *Threepenny Review,* the *Beloit Poetry Journal,* and elsewhere. Dawn designed and leads the writing program at Monson Arts and co-directs the Kauffmann Seminar on Environmental Writing. She lives in Portland, Maine.

Jessica Purdy teaches Poetry Workshops at Southern New Hampshire University. She holds an MFA in Creative Writing from Emerson College. Her poems and reviews have appeared in many journals and anthologies such as the *Museum of Americana, Poemeleon, Gargoyle, gravel, Hole in the Head Review, The Plath Poetry Project,* and *The Ekphrastic Review.* Her books include *Learning the Names* (Finishing Line Press); *STARLAND* and *Sleep in a Strange House* (Nixes Mate Books).

Paul Richmond served as National Beat Poet Laureate (2019-20) and Massachusetts Beat Poet Laureate (2017-19). He has performed nationally & internationally, from Austin Texas to Jazzköltexzeti est in Budapest, Beat Festival in Stockholm, and the Edinburgh Fringe Festival in Scotland. Paul has 6 books in print, including The 24 Hour Store was Closed. His work has appeared in many journals, magazines, anthologies, and he manages Human Error Publishing. Paulrichmond.myportfolio.com

Cheryl Savageau is the author of *Dirt Road Home* (Paterson Poetry Prize finalist and nominated for a Pulitzer Prize), and *Mother/ Land. Muskrat Will Be Swimming* was a Smithsonian Notable Book and won the Skipping Stones Book Award. Savageau has received grants from the National Endowment for the Arts and the Massachusetts Arts Foundation. She teaches at the Bread Loaf School of English at Middlebury College. Cherylsavageaublog.wordpress.com

Chelsea Steinauer-Scudder is a writer based in northern New England. As a staff writer for *Emergence Magazine*, she explores the human relationship to place. Her work has been featured in *Crannóg Magazine*, *Inhabiting the Anthropocene*, and the *EcoTheo Review*. She is currently writing her first book.

Jeri Theriault's poetry collections include *Radost, my red* (Moon Pie Press) and the award-winning *In the Museum of Surrender* (Encircle Publications). Her poems and reviews have appeared in journals such as: *The American Journal of Poetry, The Rumpus, The Texas Review* and *The Collagist*. A 2019 Maine Literary Award winner, Jeri lives in South Portland, Maine.

bg Thurston now lives on a farm in Warwick, Massachusetts. In 2002, she received an MFA in Poetry from Vermont College and she has taught poetry at Lasalle College, online at Vermont College, and currently teaches poetry workshops. Her first book, *Saving the Lamb* (Finishing Line Press) was a Massachusetts Book Awards highly recommended reading choice. Her second book, *Nightwalking*, was released in 2011 by Haleys.

Mimi White is the author of four full-length collections of poems. Her work has been honored with both the Jane Kenyon Award for Outstanding Poetry and The Philbrick Poetry Award. Her most recent book, *The Arc Remains,* is available from Deerbrook Editions and at Water Street Books. Mimi lives in an old farmhouse in Rye, New Hampshire with her dog, Scout.

Julian Wise is a junior at University of Vermont, where he is studying development, sustainable agriculture, and mathematics. Poetry, for him, is more hobby and joy.

☼

Artists' Biographies

Jason Berard has worked at Upper Valley Land Trust since March 2010 and is currently Vice President of Stewardship. He grew up in the Northeast Kingdom of VT and spent equal parts of his youth hunting, fishing, and hiking within a 30 mile radius of St. Johnsbury. After receiving a bachelor's degree in Fine Art from Boston University, he moved back to Vermont. When not at work, Jason enjoys spending time outdoors, whether on foot, bike, skis, or on the water.

Jeff Blanchard is an Athol native who enjoys hiking the great outdoors and capturing nature in photographs, with an emphasis on birds. A "birder" since junior high school, one of his goals is to photograph every species of birds in North America. The North Quabbin region is still his favorite place to explore and he is thankful for organizations like Mount Grace for preserving this precious habitat. jablanchard@yahoo.com

Natalia Boltukhova is a nomad photographer, movement coach, and linguist. She appreciates deeply the connections that form between her and all the life forms around her, and makes an effort to express the complexity of and feelings embedded in such connections. You can find more of her work on www.natalia.photography and on Instagram @ nataliaandthemountains

Martin Bridge (cover artist) Martin's work spans a wide range of media from Drawing, Painting, Sculpture, Theater Design and Site Specific Installations to Performance. He bridges realms of science and mysticism in an effort to challenge the cultural paradigms that dictate how we relate to both the natural world as well as our brothers and sisters. https:// www.thebridgebrothers.com   www.patreon.com/martinclarkbridge

Doug Brown is a former UVLT Land Steward, and current Director of Stewardship at the Berkshire Natural Resources Council in Massachusetts. Through his work and his photography he aims to connect people with the rural landscape. You can find him on Instagram @seaskymountains

Phil Brown is a lifelong birder and naturalist who has traveled extensively in search of birds and natural places, but equally enjoys exploring closer to home. He serves as Director of Land Management for NH Audubon. Phil leads bird and natural history tours and field trips for a variety of organizations, and coordinates raptor research projects for the Harris Center for Conservation Education. He resides in Hancock, NH with his wife and two young children, stewarding 22 acres.

Megan Chapman hails from a village in the heart of the Upper Valley on the Granite State side of the river. After more than a decade away, she reestablished her roots in the area where the brooks, fields, trees, and hills have always felt like home. Megan has a couple of degrees in environmental studies and enjoys learning new ways to care for our earth. Currently a Conservation Project Manager at UVLT, Megan hopes "in-perpetuity" really does mean forever!

Norm Eggert, formerly a wedding and portrait photographer, now concentrates on photographing rural New England – its landscape, towns and inhabitants. Norm and his wife Cheryl live on a small farm in northern Worcester County, where they have pet merino sheep, mini horses, and goats – all great photo subjects. Norm has taught photography for over 40 years, and currently teaches at Mount Wachusett Community College. https://normeggert.photoshelter.com/

Sherry Jennings was for 40 years a Waldorf early childhood teacher living through the seasons with young children. Since retiring Sherry has been joyfully putting purple pen to paper writing poetry and essays. She has studied Nonviolent Communication and Mediation. As a resident of Hearthstone, Sherry has the opportunity to combine in one place her love of the natural world, her interest in personal growth and conflict resolution, and her delight in writing and photography.

Alison Marchione is the Programs Director at the Upper Valley Land Trust. A Vermont native, Alison is very grateful to be able to live and work here. She finds great pleasure in connecting people to the land around them and creating accessible ways for everyone to be able to get outside. While she has created many maps in the past this is her first attempt at an artistic rendering of one by hand.

Jerry Monkman is a Portsmouth-based, award-winning conservation photographer, filmmaker, and writer, and while he has written ten books and directed two feature-length documentary films, you will usually find him shooting nature and outdoor lifestyle imagery (stills and video) for nonprofit, editorial, and commercial clients. ecophotography.com

Shelby Perry is the Wildlands Ecology Director at Northeast Wilderness Trust, where she has worked since 2016. She previously spent two years documenting and advocating for wilderness in Wyoming's Red Desert, and served terms in both AmeriCorps and the US Peace Corps, in the High Sierra in California and in West Africa, respectively. When she's not protecting and defending wilderness, Shelby enjoys exploring it on foot or through photography, science, and artwork.

Brendan Wiltse is a research scientist and conservation photographer. He holds a Ph.D. in biology from Queen's University and has worked on the impacts of climate change, road salt, and other stressors on aquatic ecosystems across northeastern North America. His photography work is focused on connecting people to wild landscapes and wildlife, while also telling the story of important regional conservation work. Brendan's work has been published in numerous regional and national publications.

☼

Land Trusts

Agrarian Trust

Nationwide

Agrarian Trust's mission is to support land access for next generation farmers. We need to chart the way forward. We need to hold our precious farmland in a trust for its best uses: sustainable food production and collective, ecological stewardship. We must also help the incoming organic leadership build on the legacy of our organic elders, many who have been farming for more than 30 years, and keep organic land in production. We need to support the stakeholders engaged in complex land succession, with all the accounting, estate planning, retirement planning and legal and technical assistance that is necessary. We need a national conversation that leads to action and traction for sustainable farming at the foundation of a new, just and equitable economy. Finally, we need community centered Agrarian Commons to create democratic ownership, tenure, and equity rooted in the land, individualized to place, and connected across the country.

Kennebec Estuary Land Trust

Bath, Maine

The Kennebec Estuary Land Trust is committed to conserving land and wildlife habitat of the Lower Kennebec and Sheepscot River estuaries. We are a volunteer-driven, donor-supported organization serving the communities of Arrowsic, Bath, Bowdoinham, Dresden, West Bath, Georgetown, Richmond, Westport Island and Woolwich. An estuary is a partially enclosed body of water along the coast where freshwater from rivers and streams meet and mix with salt water from the ocean. Estuaries and the lands surrounding them are places of transition from land to sea, providing important refuge for wildlife to feed, roam, and thrive. The Kennebec River contributes an average of six billion gallons of water to the Gulf of Maine per day, making its influence on the state's water quality and overall ecological health significant. KELT maintains twelve preserves for public enjoyment and has protected 4,100+ acres of land since our founding in 1989. Learn more by visiting www.kennebecestuary.org or calling (207) 442-8400.

Monadnock Community Land Trust

Wilton, New Hampshire

The mission of the Monadnock Community Land Trust is to hold land in trust for the larger community. We promote ecologically responsible use of that land and offer possibilities for affordable housing for low to moderate income families. Our intention is to protect the environment, promote the health and vitality of local communities, and promote diversity by offering access to land.

Monadnock Conservancy

Keene, New Hampshire

As a land trust for southwestern New Hampshire, our mission is to work with communities and landowners to conserve the natural resources, wild and working lands, rural character, and scenic beauty of the Monadnock region. We care for our conservation lands, and we engage people in ways that strengthen their communities and their connections to the land. To support our work, please visit our website to sign up for our monthly e-newsletter and make a donation today: www.MonadnockConservancy.org

Mount Grace Land Conservation Trust

Athol, Massachusetts

Mount Grace Land Conservation Trust benefits the environment, the economy, and future generations by protecting significant agricultural, natural, and scenic lands and encouraging land stewardship in northern and central Massachusetts. The core strength of Mount Grace Land Conservation Trust is our focus on collaboration to achieve significant land protection projects while actively stewarding the conservation areas we own. Our effectiveness is a function of our creative, innovative approach and responsiveness to the diverse conservation ethics held by the landowners of our region.

New England Forestry Foundation

Littleton, Massachusetts

A hike through a New Hampshire forest in the fall; a Vermont barn made from locally milled trees; and the clear, clean waters of a Maine river—these are just a few of the many gifts that New England's forests offer. Across the region, forests help reduce climate change by removing carbon dioxide from the air, while also providing local jobs, timber, wildlife habitat, clean air and water, and recreational opportunities. These benefits support a vibrant and thriving region, and New England Forestry Foundation (NEFF) works to protect forests and their benefits for future generations. Through the application of its core expertise in conserving forestland and advancing Exemplary Forestry, NEFF ultimately aims to help the people of New England to sustain their way of life, protect forest wildlife habitat and ecosystem services, and mitigate and adapt to climate change. NEFF owns and manages more than 38,000 acres of woodlands across New England, and protects an additional 1.1 million acres through conservation easements.

New Hampshire Audubon

Concord, New Hampshire

The mission at NH Audubon is to protect New Hampshire's natural environment for wildlife and for people. Founded in 1914 with an original focus on protecting and restoring migratory bird populations decimated by hunting and collection in the late nineteenth and early twentieth centuries, today's NH Audubon provides: environmental education programs throughout the state, statewide conservation research and wildlife monitoring, protection of nearly 10,000 acres of wildlife habitat in 39 sanctuaries, and environmental public policy and science-based advocacy.

Northeast Wilderness Trust

New England & New York

The lands protected by Northeast Wilderness Trust offer wild nature the freedom to flourish. On forever-wild landscapes, people take a step back and natural processes unfold freely. The 41,000+ acres of wildlands safeguarded by Northeast Wilderness Trust are places where native species can thrive and evolve. They offer resilience in the face of climate change, so that plants, animals, and fungi can move and adapt in response to rapidly changing environmental conditions. In essence, wilderness is self-willed land—the root of the word meaning "will-of-the-land." A wild place is free from human control, with natural processes directing the ebb and flow of life.

Southeast Land Trust

Exeter, New Hampshire

The Southeast Land Trust (SELT) conserves and stewards land for the benefit of people and nature in New Hampshire. SELT serves 52 towns and cities of Rockingham and Strafford counties and has conserved tens of thousands of acres since 1980, including nature preserves, hiking trails, farmland, and scenic vistas. SELT relies on its annual contributing members, committed Board of Directors, and talented staff and volunteers to keep advancing critical conservation initiatives in our region.

Upper Valley Land Trust

Hanover, New Hampshire

At Upper Valley Land Trust we provide conservation leadership, tools and expertise to permanently protect the working farms, forested ridges, wildlife habitat, water resources, trails and scenic landscapes that surround residential areas and commercial centers and make the Upper Valley a truly special place to live. We work with local conservation commissions and volunteer groups to identify and prioritize land conservation opportunities. We provide technical assistance and conservation solutions for landowners. We steward permanent agreements that conserve key properties forever. UVLT focuses its mission in 45 Vermont and New Hampshire towns in the upper Connecticut River Valley.

Valley Community Land Trust

Greenfield, Massachusetts

Valley Community Land Trust (VCLT) is a 501(c)3 non-profit organization that holds title to land, considering it neither as private nor public property, but as a sacred resource to be held in trust for present and future generations. Since 1977, when VCLT was incorporated, we have acquired through donations and purchase, over 200 acres of land in Franklin County, MA. This land has provided homes for more than 50 people and provided a base for agriculture, forestry and various cottage industries.

☼

Afterword

Writing the Land would never have come into being without the wonderful poets who contributed their craft to the project. Below is a poem created from the collective thoughts of some of the Writing the Land poets about the work they have accomplished, written while they were doing it.

Thank You Writing the Land Poets!

Voices of Writing The Land: A Zuihitsu
by Rachelle Parker

1.

(an island) over the frozen pond
in the woods outside,
both out of doors and out of our norms.

Rounded, and finite
It's got the tiniest little gardens of ground cover, lichen, mosses.

2.

When I was only a few weeks old my parents put me outside in a bassinet for my naps, even in the winter. Now, in my 92 year I still find my solace, my spirit, my soul, my words in the forest with beeches, oaks, violets and coltsfoot.

3.

Each limb of my body grows
branches to touch
Ancestors

of woodlands, sky seekers, root pillars,
Wisdom keepers
Leaf children of the forest floor
Create awareness and meld
Interwoven, yielding, strength, flourishing, precious flesh, bones,
root, stones.

Vibrant habitat,
silent, whirling,
chaotic, womb,
breathing marsh, red maple, frog, redwing blackbird, mud, rushes
and the dawn of each day.

4.

wondering,
will i find myself
again
with each step, leaving behind when and if

Invited into the tiniest universes, the shadows
guide me.

as time slips into the now
mystical. eternal.
blessed synchronicity

5.
Discovering

Waiting
snow have patience

ME!

Looking forward

To discovering my land
Honor speaks without words.
Awe.
Stillness is essential.
Fun.

Children run
between the trees, hop from stone to stone.
Shinrin-yoku, forest bathing for the mind and body.
Sit on a large stone and listen.
a red tailed Hawk, its voice a high squawk
The leaves of maples and beech are not open yet.
There is a rustle

6.

The stone lifts from my chest, there's a burbling
my veins, my lungs fill with the tang
of tree resin, of loam, of flowering plants, birthscent
and deathscents

dancing together peace, oasis of calm.

Healed

Good soil, good sweat.
A blessing during the pandemic
keeping with the seasons.
My surroundings.

7.

Looking forward
this northernmost section of native Pine Barrens, my life
Massachusetts
a necessary link

be flora and fauna, Muddy Pond imagine connections across the states
of ecology, of psychology, of history, of ethics, of science, of religion.
inside and outside simultaneously.

I am…
the past and the present with an eye on the future. Witness. Participant.
Glimpses.

The pond through the trees, partially frozen, stunning
blue

Whispering to the pond on my walk around it "I hear the silence of late
winter in your stillness with promises of spring sounds hovering below
your surface."

My blank canvas, filled with anticipation

what will form before me

Creation

In May, Muddy Pond exploded
with color and sounds and smells

Mother Nature's profound,
flourishing,
rewild,
dormant,
curious,
blue,
green,
dry
non-binary,
processes and
epiphanies

Poets who contributed to the Zuihitsu
Anonymous
Mary Brancaccio
Ann B. Day
Alice B. Fogel
Kathy Kremins
Jesse Lovasco
Rachelle Parker
Margaret R. Sáraco
Heather Wheeler

Writing the Land: 2021

Made with Google My Maps

Map Legend

 Agrarian Trust

 Kennebec Estuary Land Trust

 Monadnock Community Land Trust

 Monadnock Conservancy

 Mount Grace Conservation Land Trust

 New England Forestry Foundation

 New Hampshire Audubon

 Northeast Wilderness Trust

 Southeastern Land Trust

 Upper Valley Land Trust

 Valley Community Land Trust

Writing the Land, NatureCulture, and Honoring Nature

To find out more about the Writing the Land project:

https://www.writingtheland.org

To find out more about NatureCulture:

https://www.nature-culture.net

Purchase our previous book *Honoring Nature: An Anthology of Authors & Artists Festival Writers* from your local bookstore or bookshop.org or contact the publisher direct at paul@humanerrorpublishing.com

Acknowledgements

Lis McLoughlin and NatureCulture would like to thank all the poets and land trusts who joined this project in 2021: Thank You!

CPSIA information can be obtained
at www.ICGtesting.com
Printed in the USA
BVHW071707161221
624205BV00007B/264